Vanida's Journey

Vanida Corazon Kemaktun Plamondon

Print Edition

ISBN# 978-0-9878438-0-7

Distribution And Reproduction

Introduction

Part of the value of this journal to myself, is that I have some difficulty articulating what I want to communicate verbally, but if I take the time, I can clearly convey what I want to communicate in writing. In fact, I enjoy writing, and when I do write, it pleases me immensely.

I am Vanida Corazon Kemaktun Plamondon, born Vernon Richard Paul Plamondon. As a young adult, I was quite passionate about writing, whether or not I was writing fictional or non-fictional stories.

Unfortunately, as I grew older, and as I experienced more emotional difficulties as I became more disconnected emotionally from what makes me, me, my ability to write became more and more stunted, until I could no longer write with any decent ability at all, and no longer wanted to.

Many of the stupid things I have done in my life were the things I have done as a way of acting out when I have been experiencing emotional turmoil such as anger, frustration and depression and other emotions, I would start to move towards caring less and less about the consequences of my actions, until I was very self destructive.

Over the years, as I dealt with many of the underlying issues bothering me, I continued to keep my desire to be a woman hidden, so although I was beginning to reduce my tendency to become self destructive, I could not rid myself of the tendency, as I continued to hide and suppress a part of who I was.

Vanida's Journal came into existence, when I recognized I was on the verge of my snapping point, that I was becoming completely overwhelmed by the difficulties I experience in life, and I was beginning to care less and less about my well-being.

I saw that even though I was doing well financially, socially and most every other way, I was fighting a strong desire of wanting to be a woman. I knew that if I was doing well in life, but I was on the verge of my breaking point because of something that was bothering me, I knew I needed to face that issue head on or I was going to self-destruct and ruin my life.

I did not understand and I never before understood why I wanted to be a woman, and the adage "born in the wrong body" never rang true to me, because obviously you don't get to choose what you are born as, and no one ever will.

I had to understand why I wanted to be a woman, or I would never be able to figure out what I wanted to do, and the only thing I could think of was to sort out my feelings and write it down.

So for the first time in a very long time, I began to write, and I continued to write. I wrote the prelude and the first two parts of this story, and I understood what I wanted. I went to see the local mental health care worker and I asked for and got help.

It was a long time before I wrote anything else, as life carried on and I slowly sorted through what I learned, and began coping with the new issues I was experiencing in life. When I began to understand what I was doing, I sat down and wrote about it again. I discovered I could write again, that I wanted to, and that I was once again passionate about writing.

So let me tell you a story about Vanida Corazon Kemaktun Plamondon, who began to discover who she really was in January of 2010, let me tell you her story. Don't be afraid to laugh or cry with me, or experience any other appropriate feeling, as I open up my heart to you, the reader.

Chapter 1 – Familiarity With Pain

Pain. I'm not a stranger to pain, physical, or emotional, except that for the most part, only by empathy, dreams or memory have I experience the latter for a very long time.

I remember what it's like to experience an ear infection, root (tooth) infection, migraine, being nailed through the foot, having my hand sliced open, slamming into a brick wall by my head and landing on concrete stairs, wiping out on a motorcycle at about 40 kph on a gravel road, being in a Ford Bronco with no seat belt in a rollover, my buddy pinning my leg between a tree and the rear wheel of a three wheel ATV, flying over my bicycles front wheel (pothole) to land on cement, falling from the top rung of an unsecured ladder to land with my ankle twisted in the ladders rungs after landing with the ladder, having my legs swept out from me to be nearly knocked out landing on the floor or cement numerous times, play-fighting with friends where we actually hurt each other intentionally (I once choked a friend into unconsciousness, and a couple of other friends DDT'ed me so hard I was knocked out, threw up later, and hence they started calling me stew-pot, getting my tongue frozen to a metal tank, getting my thumb slammed in a car door, getting my bare foot slammed in car door (a couple times actually), seriously hurting my knuckles punching a door open, being smoked in the back by a baseball bat, being clipped on the head by a hockey stick, being smoked in the head by a baseball, getting bagged more times than I can remember, having my hand squeezed in a vice (on a bet), receiving minor burning by intentionally placing my hands in hot water (on a bet), playing knuckles with boards (and winning), pounding cinder-block wall until my knuckles were bloody, letting friends practice pain causing techniques learned in ninjutsu, and these are the injuries I really remember, and does not count all the lesser injuries I no longer remember, or the ones sustained while drunk (apparently, a security staff of six at my former college dorm could not subdue me during a drunk where I had alcohol poisoning).

Even through all that, I have never broken a bone, and though I appreciate the durability of my body, I don't appreciate the fact that it has led to arthritis having started plaguing me in my late twenties. Though it usually doesn't bother me other than being in varying degrees of pain on a regular basis, there were a couple of times this last year where I was in enough pain where I would just curl up in a ball and cry. The worst thing about having arthritis at a young age is knowing you will be dealing with it for a long time, more pain as I get older, and if I take good care of my health, the less bad episodes I will have, but also have a longer life span to have more life time to have arthritis.

Having experienced such a variety of pain, such pain still only holds a candlelight to emotional pain.

Chapter 2 – Who I Was

I remember with clarity, feeling like the ugly pudgy kid, I remember I ate more when things distressed me, contributing to a painful body image I fervently tried to ignore. I remember stealing and hoarding girls clothes, and the shame and dirtiness that dressing up caused me.

When I had my growth spurt, I felt like I had turned into some horrible masculine monster, I remember when I realized I looked nothing like a girl. I can still feel the pain when I burned the stash of tiny girl clothes I had that no longer fit me. I can still feel the pain when I decided there was nothing I could do about it, and decided I had to start being a man.

I could, and still can, act like a man, I stood up to the people who would push me or my friends around or would try to bully us, and despite our tight little clique being pretty nerdy, eventually everybody respected us and nobody would pick on us.

Despite my size, you really couldn't get nerdier than me. At one time or another I was in the science club, chess club, rocket club, badminton club, ping pong club, the reading club, and generally any short lived club that started up, I played casual sports during lunch hour and regularly after school during the times not allotted to the sports teams. Me and my friends also played Dungeons and Dragons on the weekends, had regular card games of various types, did a lot of hunting and camping (shooting and drinking, but we tried not to do so together as that bred unsafe stupidity).

I always knew standing up to bullying was the right thing to do, as it let the victim and bully mature positively, but it was always very emotionally painful for me. For one, it was always quite painful, and still is, whenever I needed to assert myself, even when I saw the necessity. I also found it quite painful to realize someone did not respect me unless I was tough enough to make them respect me, as I saw respect as something that would make life so much easier for everyone if it was not earned but freely given.

It was easy enough for me to see that the root of the problem for some guys who had trouble with women was simply that they did not respect women, or even worse they objectified them. Though not knowing why at the time, respecting women only seemed to make it hard for a girl to see me as anything but a friend. Having this attitude was painful for me, as I never had a girlfriend as a teen, and I new it was not manly to feel this way.

I worked hard trying to control my emotions, and it only made it worse when I lost control of them. I remember coming home to cry sometimes before I had many friends, thinking nobody liked me. I remember the homicidal bursts of anger I had against my brother when he would provoke me to beat him up, (not too long ago, I actually learned my sister thought I was protecting her from him). I remember sometimes hating life enough to want to end it.

I can still remember when girl who didn't seem to like me sat on my lap and she and the class laughed at my arousal, and I remember how much it hurt to be used that way, to be made to feel dirty, to realize I was so horny, brushing against a tree the wrong way, would arouse me. When one of my classmates grabbed my penis, I went completely ballistic on him, screaming at him for touching me that way, to say I was homophobic would be an understatement. I recognized the feelings of being violated as very emasculating, especially when I thought I should have been happy a pretty girl wanted to sit on my lap earlier.

I began to masturbate when I realized that it was the only way to sate the constant state of arousal I would have otherwise been in. I felt shame in being so weak as to not be able to control my own body, but I hated being horny even more, and I felt bad about hating something I thought I should revel in. I thought I was screwed up because I didn't want to screw every girl in sight, and I thought there was something wrong with me for wanting to find the right girl and waiting until marriage before having sex. I realized I was a closet romantic, and that bothered me just as much as anything else, because while manly men should be romantic to their women, they should not be harboring romantic fantasies such as waiting for marriage before sex, fantasizing about weddings, romantic movies about man meets woman, dream homes, what my future children would be like, what I could do to raise them to be great people, and the great things my family could do for society. To put it simply, I thought I was frakked up seriously.

To make my confusion worse, I knew I would be compelled by my own romanticism to honestly admit to a girl I might get involved with what was wrong with me, something I felt I was too cowardly to do.

I remember the first time I tried to kill myself. I had walked to our family's cabin, I had tied a rope to the ceiling rafter, climbed on to a stool, made a noose, put it around my neck, and stepped off the stool (I guess I forgot to put this on my list of physical pain I've experienced, but remembering this has nothing to do with physical pain), and when the rope started to choke me, I started to freak out and started to thrash about trying to get back on the stool. I got my foot back on the stool just before I was starting to black out. I frantically fought to loosen the noose and get it off my neck, and I don't even remember how I did it, and I fell to the floor to cry. I wanted to die, and felt even worse when I believed I was to cowardly to end my misery. I eventually cried myself to sleep. That next morning, I dug through our old clothes stashed in the shed there, until I found a particularly ugly yellow turtleneck I hated, put that on to hide the rope burn and scratches, and went home.

I've only told one person about that suicide attempt, when I was in my early twenties, when I was getting some counseling for clinical depression. The counselor actually dismissed the attempt as minor because obviously I wasn't really trying to kill myself because I didn't succeed. I knew then, that even though he seemed to be sincerely trying to help me, he was flat out full of bullshit. I know that if I had known then, how to properly hang someone, or if the stool had gotten knocked over, I would not be here today. It was painful to learn someone you were depending on to help you, wasn't going to be much help if they were going to dismiss the emotional pains you've experienced, and influenced your decisions that were leading you to the trouble you needed help with.

Eventually, in grade's 11 and 12, my final years in school, I actually had a blast. Me and my friends had formed an odd lunchroom clique, even with odd rituals like fighting over one of my buddies extra pepperonis he'd take out of his pepperoni sub, and like I said before, nobody messed with us any more, especially when the smallest of my friends, who was maybe 90 pounds soaking wet went completely postal on one of the high school bullies. I tell you, it was an amazing sight to see one of the largest guys in school actually afraid of the smallest guy in school (and that's saying a lot when our high school was 8th grade to 12th grade, having been a small community).

Just like any other cliques, we enjoyed high school parties like anybody else, and even though, unlike most nerds, we were well respected by the guys in school, it didn't seem like many of the girls respected us.

When the last semester of high school was coming to an end, it was coming to the time for the grad dance (like prom), and I didn't know who I was going to go with, but I had noticed the girl about my younger sister's age who had started hanging with us at lunch time, but how could I not notice, when no other girl gave us the time of day. I asked her, and she said yes.

We went, and even though I was aroused when we danced, I could not act on my feelings, and nothing other than having a nice time happened. We really didn't talk, I didn't know what to do, and I think she was shy, or I turned her off. Though I never told anyone, what should of been one of the best nights of my life felt like a great tragedy, and I felt like a failure because I apparently had no clue how to be a man. That severely emasculated my ego, and showed me that no matter how masculine I acted, I couldn't be manly where it counted.

Somewhat painfully, I realized I really wasn't attracted to

women, and I wondered if maybe I was gay. I realized I really wasn't attracted to men either, and it was devastating to realize I was in some kind of sexual preference limbo, because I had no idea what I was attracted to. I realized if I had simply been gay, I could just start going after men and I would start sorting out those issues later. Unable to deal with this confusion, I buried all those feelings and confusion, and decided I was probably only going to be attracted to my soul mate, and I would know for sure when I met a woman I knew I would want to spend the rest of my life with.

Though this confusion plagued me off and on for the next decade after high school, it didn't play much of a part in those years as other more serious problems engulfed my in my young and stupid phase of life.

Immediately after high school, the future looked like it could be sky's the limit, and me and a couple of friends were heading off to SAIT for school. Though at the time, college was a blast, it didn't turn out so well. I was going out drinking too much, and my poor study habits were screwing me up (I coasted through high school on brains alone, I never did any homework).

One particular night I was at my friend's apartment, and they pulled out a bottle of tequila, half a bottle of rum, and I can no longer remember what else. I remember us starting to drink, but I can't remember anything after that. The next thing I remember, was coming awake tied to a bed, in a hospital robe, curtains drawn around the bed, and a man, who seem to remember wearing a suit, was sitting in a chair at the foot of the bed. I must of still been drunk, because I honestly remember believing I had been kidnapped by the government, or some other shady organization, in order to be experimented on. I loudly and violently let the man at the foot of the bed know that and what I thought of them (even if I could remember what I was yelling, it probably is not suitable for this story), unfortunately being tied to the bed didn't let me do anything except thrash about and scream until I passed out again.

The next thing I remember was coming to to violently dry heave until I passed out again.

When I woke up again, finally come to my senses, I realized I was in a hospital, and considering how disturbing my prior memories were, I was surprised to realize I felt decently well. I was looking for my clothes when a nurse stopped by and doubtfully asked if I was all right. I told her I felt fine, and asked how I got there. She told me she didn't know how I got there, but I had been treated for alcohol poisoning. I asked where my clothes were, and she told me she didn't know, but if someone was thoughtful enough, they might of stashed them under the bed.

I got dressed, and got the nurses desk to call me a cab, and they gave me a cab voucher, and told me to keep the hospital robe I was wearing to use as a jacket since I didn't have my jacket. I had that robe a long time, and I still miss it from when I lost it, as I wore it and treated as a safety blanket when things were tough, because of how I had acquired it, it made me feel protected.

When I walked through the main doors at the dorm one of the guys looked at me and yelled "Holy CRAP man! (not his exact phrasing) You're okay!"

Surprised by his reaction, I asked him what happened, since he obviously had some idea. He told me how they had found me wandering the halls in a deranged state, six of the security guys had tried to subdue me, and when they couldn't, they called the police, and the police had came and hauled me away, which explained why I got tied to the bed.

I headed to my buddies apartment to find out how I got into the state. When he opened the door after I knocked, he yelled "HOLY CRAP, [name censored]!!! (again, not his exact phrasing) YOU'RE OK!"

When I asked what happened he told me the large amount of alcohol I had consumed, and how I got paranoid about them being demons, they were afraid and locked me out of the apartment once they had tricked me out of the apartment. Now, I remember the aftermath of this episode pretty clearly, because it had clearly demonstrated to me I had a drinking problem, and though I didn't quit for years afterward (and fell off the wagon many times when I did) the memory never left me and haunted me until I did quit.

The rest of the semester did not go well, and I failed the semester.

I didn't deal with that so well, but I eventually re-enrolled in college and I went to the Devry Institute to attend Computer Engineering. I passed the first semester, but my poor study habits, clinical depression, insomnia, and my poor sleeping habits made it difficult for me to get up at reasonable time caught up to me and I failed the second semester.

Since my landlady only rented to students, I had to get a new place, so me and one of my buddies went and got an apartment, it was a bit of a dump but it was a roof over our head. As the economy was in a recession at the time, I did not find work other then sparse temp work, and after I realized that after selling most of what I owned, and that my roommate would never come up with the dough for his half of the bills, I desperately needed to get out of the situation I was in.

In the middle of the night, I grabbed a hammer, and I went to the local mall, planning to break into a store and grab some stuff to sell. At one of the stores glass doors, I wound up and hit the door with all my might. Imagine my shock when the door not only did not break, but the steel shafted hammer had BENT. Completely stunned, I just collapsed, sitting on the sidewalk curb, and all I could do was sit there dumbfounded.

Eventually I was roused from that state when I saw the flashing lights of a police cruiser approaching. All I could think to do was stash the hammer in my backpack and hide behind a pillar. Of course when one of the officers walked around the pillar I went the wrong way and walked right in front of him, shocking the hell out of him. I don't remember exactly how the officers reacted, but the end result was me being ordered to lay on the ground, hands behind my back and me being handcuffed. The pair asked what the hell I was doing, I told them, to their complete disbelief. When they retrieved the hammer from my backpack, all they could do was laugh. I don't remember what they said, but I remember feeling I had to have been the worst criminal in all of the universe for all of recorded history.

After a short conversation I wasn't privy to, they told me they were called to check on an alarm that had went off, probably when I had struck the door, and since there had been no actual break in and entry, they were going to charge me with possession of break and enter tools.

Having never been to jail, it seemed like a surreal experience to me. I believe they brought me to the station (the entrance was an underground garage type entrance), and I was brought to some sort of waiting area. There was a woman handcuffed to the chair, I don't remember what she was saying, but she was cussing out the cops something serious. I remember someone asking if I really broke a hammer trying to break into a mall, and I told them yes. After some time I was brought to another area.

I had been enjoying a card game called Magic: The Gathering which had just came out, so I came up with a half-baked scheme to get myself to their headquarters in Renton, Washington, present my ideas for their game and apply for work with their company.

I don't remember where the Greyhound trip brought me to in Montana, but I sold everything I couldn't carry, and that's where I went. I then hitch-hiked my way across the country to get to Renton, Washington. Let me tell you, if you're even a marginally imposing guy, it's pretty long wait between rides when hitch-hiking. I almost waited a week before I got picked up for the first leg of the trip.

I made my way to the Wizards Of The Coast Offices and I gave them my ideas and my application for work. I checked back several days later and they informed me they weren't looking for any new employees. I realized then, how screwed I really was. I was in a foreign country, not sure if I could even legally work there, and I had no more money. I was sleeping in fields outside while I was there, but it was that day it finally chose to rain.

I walked until I found a local 24hrs coffee shop and I went inside. When I was sure the staff wasn't paying me any particular attention, I grabbed a coffee cup from one of the tables, and went up to the counter and asked for a refill. Cold and shivering, I stayed in one of the booths of the coffee shop overnight, and I was glad they were compassionate enough not to through me out into the rain. In the early morning hours one of the girls brought me soup and asked me how I came to be there and I told her.

That day, I wandered the area until I found a field between two warehouses, found some old palettes and made a makeshift shelter.

For about a week, I collected cans and bottles to bring to a recycling center to be able to buy fast food to get by.

After a week of this, having barely eaten anything, I gave up. I made my way to my field, crawled into my makeshift shelter and started to cry, only wanting to lay there until I died from starvation. I don't know how long I lay there after I had cried myself out, but when it had been dark for a good while, I felt a presence enter my body, and I knew at that moment, without a doubt, that there was a god, a Creator, and I could not deny his existence anymore when his very spirit had touched my soul in order to comfort me and hold me (spiritually). I began to cry again, and at some point I asked for help to be sent to me. I cried myself to sleep.

I awoke to someone addressing me. I believe he was saying hello.

I don't remember what was said exactly, but he was a police officer and he was telling me that the property owners had complained that there was someone sleeping in the fields, and he was here to ask me to leave because the property owners didn't want to be responsible.

Since that time I have grown spiritually and mentally, as I have come to recognize that there is a Creator, a greater power who has created all of existence and whom loves all of us deeply, and has a plan to deliver us from our own evil, and bring us into his loving embrace.

For a short period of time, I felt truly happy, as I had been granted some spiritual enlightenment, but it did not last. It was not long before I was shown how deeply corrupted all the worlds religions had become, and I saw that the Creator's children did not live in the world the Creator desired for us, and that we truly lived in a world of our own making, and in the same way that the children in the story "Lord Of The Flies" have created their own nightmare, we have collectively done the same.

Since that time I have done many more stupid things, as I seem to have a talent of learning life's little lessons the hard way. Despite the fact that my confusion and desire to be a woman bothered me more and more every year, I kept those feelings buried and suppressed more than ever.

Occasionally I would dress up as a woman, but that would usually end up with me spiraling into a strong depression as my perception of how ridiculous I seemed to look sunk in.

Chapter 3 - What Do I Want

It wasn't until recently when I figured out I truly wanted to be a woman. I could never figure out what I really wanted. Did I just like wearing woman's' clothes? Did I have a case of gender envy, that is, if I became a woman, would I eventually get bored and decide I wanted to become a man again? Was being a woman just a persistent fantasy, a fantasy without meaning, something I wouldn't have the willpower to act on? Was the desire to be a woman just a way to embody the qualities of my idealized mate? Did I feel like a failure as a man, so I should just become a woman? Why did I want to be a woman? What was wrong with being a man? Why was I arbitrarily assigned a gender without my input? Why was gender fixed? Why couldn't we try both genders out until we knew what we were more comfortable as? Why didn't I feel like a woman trapped in a man's body, why didn't I have that particular feeling that would make things so clear?

Obviously, with this much confusion in my head, and having not sought out professional help, I was in a state of sexual identity limbo. Until not too long ago, I didn't have the mental or emotional tools to sort out this inner conflict, but that all changed when I had an epiphany, a revelation from the Creator. It was not possible for me to resolve this inner turmoil until I understood who I am.

At first, it was difficult for me to see who I was, as all I could surmise was that I was the sum and result of my experience and choices in life. I was missing something important that was stopping me from really seeing who I was. At some point in time not too long ago, I figured out that what I was missing, what I was failing to see, was that although we are the sum and result of our experience and life choices, the other part of who we are, is our hopes and dreams. All I had to do was understand where I have been, what I have done, what choices I have made and what I have learned from them, and then look at what I hope to do, the things I want, the life I want, then I would know who I am, and I wouldn't be confused anymore.

What are my hopes and dreams?

I want to build and create things with my knowledge, my skills, and my own two hands.

I want to build a home, to live in, to entertain friends and family, and to call my home.

I want to build my home with renewable energy power sources, to be free from reliance on the grid. I want my home to be small and inviting, so it is also easy to clean and maintain.

I want fair compensation for the work I provide for others.

I want to help my friends and family when they need help.

I want someone to love, someone to come home to at the end of the day, and share my day with. I want the one I love to hold me when I'm upset, when I need comfort, or when I just want to be close. I want to share the things I build and create with the one I love. I want to laugh, I want to play, I want to do daily chores, I want to plan for the future, I want to work to solve our problems, I want to debate, I want to share feelings, I want to flirt, all with the one I love. I want to touch, caress, feel against my body, kiss, love and please the one I love. I want to share my life and my soul with the one I love.

I want to wear comfortable shoes, tight jeans, cotton underwear and a cute comfy t-shirt.

Once in while, I would like to wear a pretty dress, hot high heels, sexy stockings, lacy underwear, tasteful jewelry and hairstyle, to go out and have fun, but mostly, to feel sexy.

I want to look forward to each and every new day, with wonder and awe at the new things each day will bring, to have new experiences to look forward to.

I want to regularly experience joy again, to love and enjoy life like I haven't in a long time.

I want to be healthy.

I want to go to exotic places, and ordinary places, with someone who loves me and whom I love.

I want to learn ballroom dancing, but I don't want to lead.

I want to learn figure skating.

When I learn to skate, I want to play hockey.

I want my own workshop, equipped for woodworking, and basic metalworking, so I can tinker and create to my hearts desire.

I want to write, to tell the stories that my heart and mind are yearning to tell.

I want to be able to express myself clearly, without wondering about and searching for what I want to communicate.

I want children, and at least one daughter, so I can share with her in her childhood the things I did not get to experience.

I want to see her wonder and joy as she learns and discovers every great happy moment a child can find.

I want to be there to protect her, teach her, appease her pains, and give her guidance.

I want to hug her, hold her, smother her with love and kisses, and embarrass her in front of her friends.

I want to get her a puppy, that we can train, play with, and raise together, a puppy that will grow up to love her and protect her.

I want her to tell me how her day went, and I want to cheer her up if it wasn't all she had hoped.

I want to be there to see all the important moments in her life, her first step, her first word, her first birthday, her first friend, her first boo-boo, her first laugh, her first tooth, and so on.

I want pretty things, like a beautiful canopy bed with smooth, comfortable sheets and blanket, and a gorgeous bedroom set of dressers, with a lovely vanity and a large armoire.

I want some stuffed animals, and flowers, and other pretty things to make my room more comforting and inviting.

I want to hunt, and camp, and fish, and I want to a little cabin to enjoy such activities in.

I want pink stuff, without feeling guilty for liking pink.

I want to get married, and I want my dream wedding. I want a white, satin, strapless gown with an a-line silhouette, with a lacy bodice, with pink accents and a pink bow, with a short train, and a beautiful tiara with a gorgeous lace veil. I want a huge wedding cake, and an elegant, tasteful wedding dinner. I want my bridesmaids to wear beautiful, pink or purple, bridesmaids dresses. I want a ceremony outside, on a beautiful day, under flowered arches. I want to give myself to the one I love, in front of all the friends and family I love, and commit myself to love only the one I love for all of time. I want to show the one I love to my parents and family. I want to meet the friends and family of the one I love. I want to dance with the one I love, for the last time before we make love for the first time.

I want to share my faith, with those who care to listen, and want to fellowship with me.

I want to be a woman, so I could enjoy the things I want.

I want to tell the people I care about, that I want to be a woman, and I want them to continue to be loving and accepting of my wishes, despite any reservations or bias they may have.

I want the people I care for to be free of hurt, or shame, or anger, or pain, or negative emotion of any kind, because of what I want.

I want to continue in and enjoy woodworking, carpentry, and my idle tinkering, despite the cultural masculinity of such activities.

I want to be free from feeling like a big, ugly, hairy ape.

I want to lose enough weight, so it is possible that I could become a woman.

I want to get laser hair removal, because I hate shaving.

I want facial feminization surgery, because I want a more feminine face.

I want hormone therapy, to become more feminine.

I want SRS, because I want to be a woman.

I want my own breasts, but I don't want big breasts.

I want to believe that before my time is up, the creator will bless me and allow me to attain all my dreams.

Finally, I want to be me, I want to be the me that I have been trying to hide for all my life.

When I looked at everything I wanted, what my hopes and dreams were, it became obvious to me, that if I wasn't working to fulfill all my hopes and dreams in my daily life, I was stopping myself from being me. I also became aware, from experience, that if I sought out a dream, and it didn't work out, it didn't mean I had wasted my time, or that I wasn't being myself by working for that dream. Whether or not the dream is attained, or whether or not the dream turns out to be something one is not comfortable with living with has little to do with being oneself. Working to attain one's dreams is what makes us be who we are, regardless of what the final outcome.

I understood then, the importance of the real life experience, to those experiencing gender confusion, such as myself. I now know that until I go through the real life experience, I will never resolve to a satisfactory degree, my gender confusion. To understand that I want to be a woman, and work towards that goal, will allow myself to be who I am, regardless of whether or not in the end I decide I truly am more comfortable as a woman, or I was experiencing some sort of fantasy.

Knowing this, then, all I need to do, is act on my needs, and start working towards what I want, to start truly being me. I need to seek counseling I need to start dealing with my body image issues. I need to start working on my body's health to start bringing it closer to my heart's desire. I need to come out to my loved ones and deal with the repercussions, if any. I need to start living as a woman, when I'm ready to take that step. I need to start hormone therapy when I'm ready for that. I need to start working to fulfill all my dreams.

I don't know when I'll be ready to take the first step, to come out to my loved ones. As I have been starting to understand who I am, I have just recently begun to reconnect with my emotions.

I am afraid. How will my parents react? How will my brother and sister react? How will the rest of my family react? How will my employer react? How will the community react? Can I take it if any of those whom I love won't accept what I want or ostracize me? Will the Creator bless me with the strength to endure what hardships coming out may entail? Am I making a mountain out of a mole hill? How do I come out? How do I spare myself and my loved ones unnecessary pain?

I had thought the ability to experience genuine emotion had escaped me, and as I reconnect to my emotions, it terrifies me and saddens me. A few times since I started to reconnect to my emotions, I have had moments when I just wanted to lie down and cry.

As this overwhelming emotional pain seized me, I begun to write this story, about how I came to this point. The first ending to this story was a fictional ending to a true story, because if the option were available to magically become a woman presented itself in real life, I would have taken it, regardless of consequences.

At first, writing this was a way to deal with that, unexpected, emotional pain. As I wrote, the things I was just beginning to understand about myself, sorted themselves out, and the emotion subsided, to be replaced with contentment, another emotion I have not experienced in a long time.

At this moment, I have actually lost about 15 pounds, since I consciously started trying to lose weight, and I feel healthier and actually feel happy (it feels like I opened some kind of emotional floodgates). More importantly, I look in the mirror, and I don't feel as much like a big hairy ape, and I see that there might really be a woman hiding in my reflection, struggling to come free.

As I begin this journey, to reconnect with who I am, I am sharing this story so that others could learn from my experience, to know that the only escape from one's confusion of their personal identity (this is not exclusive to the transgressed) is to become a sociopath, and trust me when I tell you, you don't want that. I realize now, discovering who we are involves trying the things we dream about, and acting on the things that engender confusion in our minds and emotions.

To deny that, is to deny who you are, or may become. I am not saying, however, that making ones life choices in order to be true to oneself does not result in hardship, pain, and conflict, because it does. It also results in personal growth, joy and maturity. Believe me, denying one's self does not spare you any hardship, pain, and conflicts, but it does guarantee unwarranted pain and misery, with lesser personal growth, joy and maturity.

I also intend to share this story to those I will be looking to for help on my path to (hopefully) womanhood. I have difficulty trusting a professional, who may or may not be able to be up to the job of providing the mental and emotional assistance I seek. They can read this story and know where I've been and where I want to go, and have a decent idea if they can provide me with the life tools and support to continue on my journey.

Finally, I want the ones I love to read this story, before I face them about what I want. I don't know how they'll react. I am starting to understand that I am afraid of how they'll react, that they won't love me anymore, that they won't understand how I am starting to feel, or won't try. I am afraid that when I need them, they won't be there. I am afraid they'll read this story and they will think I am a monster, a freak. I am afraid because I don't know how any one person will react.

I fervently hope and pray I have been making a mountain out of a mole-hill.

As I have begun writing this journal (for lack of a better description) I am reading a caregivers story by E.E. Nalley, Guardians of the Gates of Madness, and it moves me emotionally in a way that I haven't expected. The spacers of the caregivers company undergo a process that makes them female, completely, even able to have children. Mentally and emotionally I know that the current normal means to become a member of the opposite sex is a difficult and time consuming process, but if I do so, I still will not be able to birth children from my own body. I am beginning to feel quite a bit of emotional pain in knowing that is not a possibility for me, and will likely remain an impossibility in my lifetime.

If there was a way to become completely, truly female, I would jump at the chance, damn the consequences. I'm not sure why I want the ability to become pregnant, and I don't exactly understand why it's so painful to know that isn't likely to happen in my lifetime.

Chapter 4 – New Conundrums, Life Goes On

It has been a long time since I have started to write this journal, and many things have happened.

I have went to see the mental health care worker in my small community, and even though it was very difficult for me to do so, I told her I wanted to be a woman and I was coming to her to get help, before I completely fell apart emotionally and mentally and did something I regretted (again).

I have only felt the feeling of complete terror only a handful of times in my life, and as I sat there in her office, struggling to tell her why I was even there to see her, that is the feeling that unexpectedly overcame me. Fortunately she was quite understanding, and as she reassured me that I could tell her what I wanted to get help for, I began to tell her I was there to get help for a problem I had been keeping buried a long time, and I eventually told her I wanted to become a woman, all the time fighting my urge to escape and never expose my vulnerability.

When I told her, even though I was an emotional wreck, I felt as though a huge burden had been lifted. For the first time in my life, someone else knew my secret, and I could start on the path to allowing myself to be completely, truly, me.

Since then, I have been to see her to talk about my goals and plans, and recently I have been to see her and the local doctor, to tell the doctor what I wanted to do, and to ask him to look into hormone treatment for when I am ready to start hormones. Additionally, I am on the list to see the psychiatrist when he visits the community, so that I can begin to undergo evaluation on a regular basis, such that whenever I become ready for the next stage in my treatment, the evaluations and referrals I would require would be available as needed.

Surprising myself, as it turns out, the help and treatment I am seeking, has not been as important to me as actually going to get help and treatment, that getting medical help has not been as important to me as actually deciding to stop hiding parts of me, and embracing those parts of myself that I have denied and becoming wholly myself. I'm not saying I no longer want to be a woman, and in fact I want to be a woman more than ever, but I have come to understand that becoming a woman is not the goal, but rather, fully embracing who I am, who I have been, and who I want to be, is what I truly want.

A dream I recently had best illustrates the conundrum I am in. As is usual in most of my dreams, I was a woman, and I attacked a savage wolf, bent on destroying it. I fought the wolf with every ounce of my being, mortally wounding it and driving it off, but not before it tore me open, ripping apart my breasts, and destroying my genitalia, and I awoke from the dream just as I lay on the ground, dying.

At first, I thought that the dream was about me trying to destroy my volatile anger, and that it in turn destroyed me. I realized after truly trying to understand the dream, that the wolf represented my masculinity, and that if I truly tried to destroy it, I would in turn also destroy myself and my femininity.

I felt that the Creator was trying to tell me if I tried to destroy my masculinity, I would end up destroying myself and my femininity. This of course caused me to, again, question if I was making the right decision, by deciding to pursue the goal of becoming a woman.

Fortunately, I have come to learn, that like the Creator, whose image we are created in, that we are all male and female, and generally men are more male than female, and woman are more female than male, and though embracing the femininity and masculinity opposite ones birth gender may rise in insecurities, it would be trivial for most men who are mostly male and most women who are mostly female.

Personally, I feel that there are less female to male transgendered people, because it is more socially acceptable for women to embrace masculine traits, than it is for men to embrace feminine traits.

Of course, I now had to look within again, and decide if I was more female than male.

Unfortunately, I could not come up with a truly objective way of determining if I was more male or more female. As this issue caused me to question if I really wanted to be a woman or not, I was getting quite frustrated.

Eventually, I figured out that the answer was within the question itself. The answer could only be determined by embracing my Femininity and Masculinity, and seeing what I was comfortable with. Even though in my heart I am one hundred percent certain that I can only be myself by becoming a woman, I still have to embrace what masculinity I have.

As a quick example, both the mental health worker and doctor wanted to know if I wanted to still be a carpenter if I became a woman. I enjoy carpentry and woodworking, and I don't want to give up the trade, even though the trade is a somewhat masculine trade. Though I often fantasize about being a secretary or a nurse, I see that many aspects of those careers, are things I could not personally handle very well, and I do not wish to.

So in other words, to answer the question, I just have to be female, without giving up the masculine traits that are part of me, and the answer will present itself. There is no need for me to know the answer now, as the answer will become clear and apparent when I go through the real world experience.

Already I have some idea of what the answer is, though I have no way to be certain, because though I have had no luck in the past losing weight in order to become more feminine, I have been slowly and steadily been losing weight ever since I have decided to seek help, because I am now acting on what I want, what I want is part of who I am, I am embracing who I am, male and female, and I have begun to believe I can be female if I want to, and I want to with all my heart.

These questions of femininity and masculinity bring me to my second conundrum. I could move to a large community like Edmonton, and I could change my identity, and I could become a woman anonymously, or I could remain in my small community and go through my transition openly, without hiding it from the community.

If I go through the anonymous route, I cut myself off from friends and family, and I put myself alone in the world, always keeping a secret that is always at risk of being revealed anyway. If I go through the transition openly, then I will be subject to discrimination, ignorance and various other hardships, but I don't have to remove myself from my friends, family, and community.

I have decided I am going to go through my transition openly, mostly because I value my friends and family, and I'd rather be subject to discrimination, ignorance and various other hardships, than cut myself off from my friends and family, even though I may be at the receiving end of such things from some of my friends and family.

In small part, I want to go through my transition openly, because I believe if society was more open to men and women embracing their masculinity and femininity, I might not have had as many difficulties in my life, because I might have been less likely to act out in destructive ways, because I might have embraced my femininity.

Chapter 5 – A Good Friend

When one moves to a new community, even if one has much family there, one usually doesn't have any friends there and must make new friends, which is the situation I found myself in when I moved to my mother's home community.

I have made friends with much of the people I know here in my community, and I have become good friends with a couple of my cousins, one who is my coworker, and one who I become close friends because I helped her out and I ended up telling her that I wanted to become a woman, because I desperately wanted someone to talk to about womanly things, and she has ended up helping me out immensely, just by being someone I could talk to about what I'm going through, and whom I could be myself around.

Oddly enough, it started when someone vandalized her TV satellite dish, and threatened her family, because as the local postmaster, they thought she was stealing their mail. Of course they waited until her husband was out of town and she was more vulnerable.

Messing with any of my family is not something I like, so I started crashing on her couch and staying with her on the weekends when her husband wasn't home so she would feel safer. Of course, when there, we would talk about the situation, and she would vent to me about the things in her life that was bothering her.

Truth be told, when someone wants to vent, and share their problems, I want to listen and be a metaphorical shoulder to cry on, because that's what women do, and of course I want to be woman. I also know a woman isn't looking for a solution, she just wants to vent. Of course, if there are obvious or workable solutions to the problems, I will present them when the time is right. I don't know if the last part is part of women do, because I have to date only two close woman friends.

I do know, generally, that when a man vents, he's usually really saying; "I got a problem, can you help me figure it out?", and it seems to me when a women vents, she's really saying; "Somethings bothering me, will you listen?"

I don't usually like it when guys vent their problems to me, because it feels like a lot of pressure to come with solutions to their problems, when they still need to work out the solutions for themselves anyway.

I feel more myself when a woman shares her problems with me, because there is no demand to do anything other than listen, and reaffirm that what she is thinking is right, and she is not being ridiculous, or mean, or bitchy, or anything else, for thinking such. I know just by listening and allowing herself to sound out her problems, she is going to work them out for herself. Sometimes, I have to point out the obvious, so she can get on the right track.

Needless to say, very few men share their girlfriend/wife/other problems with me, since I'm going to side with the women most of the time anyways.

So yeah, when a woman wants to vent their feeling to me, I'm going to listen, because it makes me feel more like the real me, so when my cousin started to vent her feelings to me, I listened, even if she had to talk til three in the morning (which she did, sometimes).

I hope, that by listening, it helped her out, though I am not sure by how much. She did figure that she needed to find another job if she could not count on having a safe work environment, and the other things bothering her are between herself and her husband and kids so of course that's probably going to bother her for awhile until she can work that out between herself and them.

After awhile, I started to go to her place because I wanted to. It started to feel like I was going for a sleepover, and it was kinda like a girls night. I really started to want to tell her what was going on with me, because I started to really want to tell people; "Wait, this is not really me, this is me!"

Of course I was afraid to tell her, because I was afraid of how she would react, and I didn't want to alienate one of the few close friends I made since moving to the community.

Surprisingly, it wasn't anywhere near as hard to tell her as it was to tell the community mental health worker, and I ended up blurting it out. Although she seemed a little surprised, it really didn't seem to bother her.

Happily, having someone to confide in, to be myself around, has helped me immensely and I have been starting to feel much better about myself, and I am finding it easier to confront my negative body issues, more specifically I no longer feel like a big hairy ape, or a fat whale, which she tells me is an issue that many women have to confront, so I also don't feel like a freak for having felt that way. It seems it has been easier to deal with such issues when I have a peer who can emphasize or understand what I am feeling.

I have also demonstrated for her my female voice I am working on, and I could practice at her place, but so far I have been getting nervous enough that it's difficult.

I doubt that her perspective, or any other woman's perspective, is closer to my perspective than the male perspective, but at least I am learning that some of the ways I think are not unusual (YAY!!! I'm not a mutant, oddball, freak.). Obviously some of the ways I think are not very female.

For example, I don't really want breasts, but if I'm going to take hormones I'm going to get them anyway, so because I want to be female more than I don't want breasts, I'm going to get breasts, but I don't think I'm going to get breast augmentation, even if they turn out really small.

Of course, my cousin tells me I have got to have breasts for some clothing to look right, and I really like pretty clothes, and when I visualize breasts, then I kind of start to see them as cool fashion accessories, and then I get mortified that I want lumps of flesh on my chest so I can look pretty, so NOT the right motivation for getting breasts. Then I remember one of the reasons I want to be female is that I want to be pretty, and then I start to wonder if wanting to be pretty is a good reason to be motivated to do anything.

Point is, I think my perspective is a mishmash of typically female and typically male perspectives, but I have been exposed to the male perspective all of my life, and not any female perspectives, so when I think in a way not typical for my peers, it has been very easy for me to feel alienated and confused.

It has been nice to finally have a friend to be able to ask; "Is it strange to think this way?"

Chapter 6 – An Emotionally Tough Weekend

When I went to check my mail on Friday, I found that some panties and a halter top that I ordered had come in, but that they hadn't been sent to the shipping address I specified, that is c/o my cousin, so that I wouldn't have to undergo the embarrassment from postal workers knowing about me buying woman's clothing and intimate wear.

It dawned on me then, it would be possible that people might start to suspect embarrassing things about myself, such as my wearing woman's clothes, before I was ready to reveal to the community my desire to be a woman. Despite my desire to undergo my transition openly to the community, I didn't feel ready or strong enough to "come out of the closet" so to speak.

I found it quite devastating when I realized that I might be forced to reveal to my friends and family that I want to be a woman before I was planning to do so and before I felt ready to do so. Needless to say, I was a little depressed by that fact.

Still feeling down, I decided that since I had some new under wear and a new halter top, and I also got in a new pair of jeans, I might as well try my new clothes on. Somewhat less hindered by negative body issues than ever before, I really, truly felt sexy, regardless of what my actual appearance may have been.

Laying in bed, really feeling sexy, I suddenly knew, without a doubt, that in that state of mind, that if anyone, even a total stranger, approached me and asked to have sex with me, my first thought would be YES!!! Just the thought of feeling desirable made me understand, that if someone ever honestly wanted me in that way, that I would completely want to please them in any way I could, and I would really want them sexually.

That feeling really scared me, because I have never been really sexually attracted to anyone in my life, and then I learn that not only can I be sexually attracted to anyone, but that I was afraid of even being able to exert self control if I ever experienced such an attraction to anyone specific.

I have read many stories of transsexual woman giving themselves over to men they fall in lust with, to the point of letting themselves be used in any manner possible, even in painful and humiliating ways. I found this idea difficult to comprehend, since I found it hard to believe that a woman who should have known better, could let themselves be used that way.

Having been exposed mostly to a male perspective for most of my life, I just wasn't equipped to understand being sexually aroused by feeling sexy or desirable. All my life I thought sexual arousal came from desiring someone in a sexual way, and I in fact was completely alienated by my apparent lack of sexual desire.

Not knowing I would get sexually aroused if I felt desirable, and having never felt desirable before, I really had no way of knowing what was wrong with me.

Of course I'm going to have to be cautious if I ever enter a relationship, and learn more about myself if I want to avoid becoming excessively promiscuous, though I'm not really sure if that's a bad thing, and I doubt anyone I get involved with would think it's bad either.

I eventually fell asleep feeling pretty good about my self, although I was a little afraid of wanting to have sex with everything with two feet and a heartbeat, even though I thought that was really unlikely.

When I woke up, I took a good look at myself, and I was completely grossed out by how hairy I was and I began feeling like an ugly hairy beast, and it made me really want to cry, though I couldn't. I desperately wanted to wear the clothes I wanted to wear, I wanted to wear panties and tights, and jeans and a cute top. I didn't want to feel like a big ugly freak any more. I curled up in bed and I hugged myself and just felt really, really awful. I wished I had a big teddy bear to hug, and I desperately wanted someone to hug me and make me feel better.

Eventually I couldn't stand feeling so sorry for myself, and I didn't want to be a major downer when I went over to my cousins place later that morning for pancakes, so I got up and I was going to do something about how I felt.

I went to the local stores to see if they had any Nair, but neither store opened until noon, so I was out of luck. I went to where I have some of my stuff stored and picked up what I had for woman's clothes, some underwear, some hosiery, a nighty and a dress. I went home and I began to shave my body. It took me two hours but I immediately felt much better, having done something about how bad I felt.

I decided than that I was going to wear panties and tights from then on, since it was unlikely that anyone was going to figure out what I was wearing under my jeans, especially when I was wearing my coveralls for work as well. I got dressed, then I left to go to one of the local stores to pick up a couple of things I needed.

Halfway to the store I suddenly became self-conscience and realized I never checked my jeans for holes and I started to freak out thinking people might figure out I was wearing panties and tights. It's moments like that one that make me really want to shout out to the world "HEY! I WANT TO BE A WOMAN!!! I'M GOING TO WEAR THE CLOTHES I WANT!!!"

With every day that passes, it becomes more and more obvious that, not only does it become harder and harder to hide my desire to become a woman, I really don't want to hide anymore.

I am torn between jumping into everything involved with becoming a woman, telling friends and family, taking hormones, living as a woman, and getting surgery, and a prudent notion that I should be absolutely sure of what I truly want before action.

I'm not saying I'm having second thoughts, because I haven't yet, but the fact of the matter remains that I haven't had many female friends, so I don't have much exposure to the female perspective and I don't know a good deal of what it is to be a woman.

I'm pretty certain I want to be a woman, because in reality, I want to be who I truly am, and I believe that I really am a woman. I know for sure, that typically, most men don't want many of the things that I want, and typically they're things that women want. Of course, I'm probably not as female as most woman, but I'm okay with that.

The other caveat is that some of the feelings, experiences, thoughts, or other aspects of being a woman may take me by surprise and cause me difficulties I don't expect or are prepared for. My feelings I experienced when I felt desirable illustrates the dangers I may find myself in, as it's pretty easy for me to see myself getting in a very bad situation if I got into a relationship and let my feelings control my actions.

Of course this frightens me somewhat when I realize hormones will cause me to become more emotional, and as I am currently opening up and beginning to no longer suppress my emotions and understanding what it is like to begin to deal with thoughts and feelings I don't expect or are not prepared to deal with, I know that hormones are going to be a lot of dealing with unexpected thoughts and feelings, and I would like to be prepared to deal with them.

Though I could be taking hormones right away, I figured that since I started to be true to myself, I should deal with the emotions I am no longer suppressing, and begin to understand who I am inside.

Chapter 7 – Fire!

Oftentimes in life you get hit with the unexpected, especially when you're not prepared for it. It's really not fun, but it's not like anything can be done to change what's happened, and all I can do is carry on as best I can, and hope that life's little curve balls aren't going to be tragedies.

Monday after work, I had just gotten home, and I wasn't doing anything all that interesting other than surfing the net. My aunt told me we were expecting a couple of my cousins and their kids for supper, and she was going to get some stuff for supper (I was living with my aunt and uncle, as me and my aunt both worked for my cousin's company).

I was about to doze off, when I heard my aunt yelling from the doorway at me and my uncle. At first I hadn't any idea what she was yelling. I came out of my room and she told me the garage, which is attached to the duplex we live in, was on fire, and asked where our fire extinguisher was.

I told her I didn't know where it was, and I went and grabbed the mop bucket and started to fill it in the bathtub. When it was full I put the trash can in the tub to fill with water, grabbed the pail and headed to the door. My uncle was dressed and standing by the door, so I handed him the pail and grabbed a bucket to get more water. I dumped the water in the trash can into the bucket, put the can back in the tub to fill, grabbed the bucket and headed to the garage.

When I walked into the garage, I saw flames and smoke in the office there, so I held my breath and walked into the room. Very quickly I found I no longer could see and I was soon forced to take a breath. My lungs were burning, I couldn't see and I was on the verge of passing out, and I knew if I did I would die. I flung the water in the general vicinity of where I saw the fire and got out of the garage as quickly as I could.

As my vision cleared up I saw many empty fire extinguishers sitting on the ground outside, and I told those outside helping that it was no longer safe to enter the garage. I looked inside and I saw much larger flames coming out of the office.

Knowing that the duplex garage was full of fuel, oil, and many flammable materials, I knew the building was going to go up in flames very rapidly, I went back to our unit to retrieve the bare essentials before it became to dangerous to do so.

I grabbed the batteries and charger for my cordless tools for work, and I brought them outside. I saw my coworkers, who were staying in the unit between ours and the garage while they were in town working, grabbing their stuff from the unit beside the garage.

I went back into our unit and I retrieved my work clothes and boots, my outdoor clothing, my laptop and my hard drive, and a laundry hamper of clean clothes. Smoke was beginning to leak into the unit and I told my aunt and uncle that it wouldn't soon be safe in there.

I stopped and watched as the fireman had arrived and were unrolling their hoses and preparing to fight the fire. One water truck was being hooked up to the fire truck and another was positioning itself to deliver some water. By this time the flames were flowing out of the garage entrance and my heart sank.

I moved my aunt and uncle's propane barbecue and my storage boxes away from the building, and then me and my aunt and uncle went to put our stuff in her SUV. Not knowing what else to do, I went to join the crowd watching the fire. My cousin, whose duplex it was, was crying, and my aunt was trying to calm her down.

I went to see how my uncle was doing, and my cousin whom I have become good friends with was bawling her eyes out. I remembered she had been telling me the previous day that her eyes were bugging her the way they would when something bad was going to happen. I asked her what was wrong and she told me she just recently had a dream that her mother had been shot.

I turned to see how the firefighters were doing, and they had got one hose going and they were using it to wet down the fuel tank just outside the garage. Just as they were getting a second hose going, we could see smoke starting to come out of the roof as the fire was getting into the roof.

My knees almost gave out as I realized they weren't going to be able to save the building and my stuff in my room wasn't going to be saved. I could only watch and I just wanted to lie down, curl up and cry. A few times as we were watching, I almost fainted.

After awhile I heard the sound of tracks from heavy equipment down the road and I saw the backhoe from work coming down the road. I was so relieved when I figured out they might have a chance to save our unit.

My aunt was telling my cousins all the kid's were safe and at my cousin's house, and started to gather everyone up to head to her house. I came, not able to bear watching anymore. We brought what stuff we grabbed inside and started to sort ourselves out.

My cousin's daughter started cooking some fries, and me and my uncle started to cook soup. I reminded my cousin to make some arrangements for my coworkers who had been in the unit between ours and the garage. While there one of my other aunts offered to let me stay with them, and I told her I probably would.

My aunt and my cousin left to go make arrangements for my coworkers and get a hold of the insurance company through their emergency number. They asked me to stay and help watch the kids.

While there, one of my nieces climbed on my lap and asked what's wrong. I asked her what she meant and she said she climbs on my lap and I push her off saying "not a couch". I told her sorry, but uncle's a little sad and not really in the mood to play.

After awhile, when I saw my uncle had things under control at the house, I decided to go check on a couple of my other cousins, knowing that probably nobody had checked on how they were doing. I found them keeping an eye on the duplex.

I checked on them and how the firefighters were doing at the duplex. They were fine and the firefighters had gotten the fire out and by one of my coworkers having ripped the duplex in half with the backhoe they had saved the last unit where me and my aunt and uncle had been living. I knew for sure then that everyone was fine and our stuff was going to be fine.

My legs started to shake, and I had to sit down or I was going to fall. I sat on the ground and I began to cry. My cousins began to comfort me and after a bit one of them asked if I had called my parents yet and told them what happened. I told her no, and she offered to let me use her phone to call them. She dialed the number and told my mom I wanted to talk to her and passed me the phone.

I said hi a few times over and over and I began to cry again and handed the phone back to my cousin as I realized I was becoming incoherent. She talked to my mom for a bit while I was sobbing, and when I was done crying I talked to her and told her what happened. When she was talking to me she asked me why I had been so upset and I told her I had gotten scared.

After talking to her for a bit, I talked to my dad and filled him in on what happened, and after talking to him for awhile, my mom told him she wanted to talk to me again, as apparently I was somewhat incoherent.

Chapter 8 Fire! Continued

I had not finished the previous chapter until now because I could not figure out why I was so upset about the fire until just recently.

For most of my life I rigidly suppressed and controlled my emotions, even to the point that at times I would have a self destructive rage building up threatening to overwhelm me. Looking back, I wonder why I was diagnosed in the past with antisocial personality disorder, in which for the most part I fit the symptoms, but for that anger and rage.

Now I believe that by suppressing my emotions and ignoring a huge part of my being, I was becoming equivalent to some type of functioning sociopath, but I was frustrating my mental well being and that frustration was fueling that anger over time. Even though I continued to improve my ability to control, divert and deflect my anger, and worked hard to channel that anger creatively, it always continued to build up over time.

I know with certainty that if I had not broken down and decided to try and figure out what was wrong with me and do something about it, I would have self-destructed in some manner.

As I began to recognize and embrace the parts of myself I had tried to excise from my being I believe I was dealing with the root of that anger and it began to fade away.

I did not know why I reacted the way I did when the fire happened because I was used to reacting to such an event with anger at losing my home, frustration at being forced to deal with the consequences of the unwanted situation forced upon me, and rage at being forced to take a step backwards in my plans.

That, of course, is not what happened to me.

At the time I did not even recognize the feelings I was experiencing, as it was like I was somewhat emotionally detached from my body, something I don't recall ever happening to me before, and when the night's events came to an end, all the emotions hit me at once and that's when I collapsed in an incoherent, babbling mess.

I had been scared when I tried to help out with putting out the fire, I got stressed out with the possibility of losing some of my stuff, stressed out with suddenly becoming homeless, I got scared for the possibility of harm coming to my relatives, I felt hurt that my home would be taken away from me, I became afraid for what would happen to me, and I simply became terrified by how suddenly everything in my life could be changed and how little control I actually I had.

For the first time, that I can recall anyway, I was scared shitless, terrified. I broke down because I did not react like I ever have before, and I was not equipped with the mental tools to deal with those emotions.

As traumatic as the fire turned out to be for me, I would not change anything because my reaction to the fire was an emotional breakthrough. For the first time in my life, I was reacting emotionally, with appropriate emotions.

I still get angry, but my anger has seemed to become fairly simple to deal with, and since sometime after the fire I have been at peace with myself for the first time in a long time.

Sometimes, I feel like a child again, as it feels like I am looking upon the world with eyes I haven't used in a very long time. I did not even realize this until one day my father was telling me about his amazement at my wonderment, curiosity and my analysis of the woodworking techniques used in a hand built airplane in the Aeronautic Museum in Edmonton.

Nowadays I feel a bit betrayed that most of the mental health professionals have been unable to help me in any useful, constructive way, but I am not angry at them anymore. I am not surprised because mental health professionals seem to approach therapy as a tool they use to help a patient, when the reality is that only the patient can help herself, and the mental health professional should be working to teach and pass on to the patient the mental tools they need to help themselves.

Chapter 9 – Life Beyond Gender Identity Crisis

A Letter To The Editor; My life does not revolve around wanting to become a woman, and as an example here is a letter, before shortened and summarized for publication by the Edmonton Journal and Nunatsiaq News, and as it appears on my blog. Note that I am greatly exaggerating for effect the hardship I am undergoing.

Living In Nunavut – The Dream Become Nightmare

Last night, for the first time in awhile, I curled up in bed, and I cried myself to sleep. I have come to live in a dream, which has become a vivid nightmare, a harsh reality, from which some facing such a reality, would never find escape.

I came to Kugluktuk, Nunavut a couple of years ago, to live and work, because as an Inuk, Nunavut was a sort of a "Promised Land" for the Inuit people. It represented all the hopes and dreams of the Inuit people as a place in which the Inuit people could call their own, where we would have access to the same education available to all others in Canada, we would have plenty of available work, affordable housing and ample assistance to be able to build our own homes.

Though I was raised elsewhere, I have plenty of family in Nunavut, and I have always wanted to reconnect with my roots.

Not long after the creation of the land of Nunavut, and although I had already established myself in a good trade (I was an experienced cabinetmaker managing a custom kitchen manufacturing shop) I longed to see Nunavut, and the temptation and desire to actually move there to live and work increased exponentially each year.

Having been outright told by the Nunavut Government that the GN (Government of Nunavut) was actively seeking qualified or experienced Inuit beneficiaries (which I was) to come work for the GN, I applied for every single position that became available that my experience qualified me for, for many years, and I applied for all entry level positions in any field in which I had even the slightest interest. Many government officials and politicians even went as far to say that they could not find enough qualified or experienced Inuit beneficiaries.

I do not hesitate to say, that when saw that the GN was beating their chests crying out; "Where are you, those that I have set out a place for, come in and take up your seat, the one I have set aside for you, and partake in the bounty I have prepared for you.", I eagerly came to their door, and I knocked, I presented myself, and I declared that I had come to answer my summons, and all that greeted me was stone dead silence.

I did not limit my job search to government positions, and in the private sector I was overwhelmed and bombarded with job offers, but without the availability of housing, I was unable to take any of the jobs offered. I could almost literally see the frustration seething from their pores, and they all confirmed that as I had been told, there was no shortage of work available in Nunavut.

In retrospect I should have realized then, that everything I was seeing, was not necessarily as it seemed.

To this day, I have yet to be interviewed for any position by the GN, but to be fair, I have recently stopped applying for work with the GN since moving to Kugluktuk, having come to work in Kugluktuk in a trade I was happy to be in.

A couple of years ago, the opportunity to come to Nunavut to live and work finally presented itself. I was in Kugluktuk for my grandmothers funeral, and I happened to ask my cousin if he was looking for employees, and paraphrasing his answer, he pretty much said: "Can you start Monday?"

At the time, I wasn't sure if I wanted to pull up stakes and move to Nunavut just like that, but I had been working as a kitchen installer at the time, and I was in a very tight spot financially, since several of the kitchen manufacturers I worked for had gone bankrupt and went out of business, leaving me unpaid and in some financial trouble.

After careful thought I realized that Alberta was ripe for another recession and as it was not an ideal place to be between jobs, I decided I might as well move to Kugluktuk, especially since my boss was going to help me find a place to stay, the one barrier that was proving nearly insurmountable.

I moved in with my aunt and uncle living in one of the apartments of the duplex he owned, and as we only had to pay utilities and food, it was very affordable.

After working that spring, I finalized my decision to move completely to Nunavut after conducting enough research to find that the GN had programs in place to aid Inuit beneficiaries in getting affordable housing, help to purchase a home, renovate a home or build a home.

It appeared that food and fuel was subsidized, programs

existed to help equip hunters, carvers, tradesmen and local business, acquisition of land to lease to build on from the municipality was reasonable and affordable, and shipping by barge was subsidized. Add to all that, my boss agreed to sign me on for a carpenter's apprenticeship.

Even Internet did not appear to be a problem, as Northwestel was offering a fairly new satellite Internet option by the name of Netkaster, which was actually a service Northwestel was reselling from Telesat, the same company that many satellite providers like WildBlue in the United States were using to provide such service, with which most customers were having a positive experience.

Looking at all those possibilities, it seemed that moving to Nunavut was a no brainer. I borrowed money from my parents and I returned to Alberta to crate my stuff to send up to Nunavut, and get rid of my truck and all the belongings, such as some of my tools, that I could not afford to bring up to Nunavut. It took me most of the summer to repay my parents and pay for the freight, but as my intention was to move to Kugluktuk permanently, I wasn't concerned with the expense.

Seeing all the shipping crates being brought up by the Nunavut Housing Corporation for their housing projects, that was available to me to take apart to gain good sound plywood due to my job, I began gathering plywood and I applied for a lot from the municipality so that I may eventually build my own house. I looked into the Material Assistance Program available from the Nunavut Housing Corporation and found I would not qualify for the program until I had lived in Nunavut for two years and I planned accordingly.

All in all, that first summer held such promise, and it was fairly easy to believe that Nunavut was indeed well on it's way to becoming a land of promise for the Inuit people, that the Nunavut Land Claims Agreement was truly bringing about a golden age for the Inuit people.

Unfortunately, in that first winter I lived there, my health almost crushed all my hopes and nearly broke my spirit. As I had already been experiencing joint pain to varying degrees before moving to Nunavut, and though, for Kugluktuk, the winter was somewhat mild, the colder climate introduced me to more frequent and more severe episodes of joint pain.

Needless to say, I did not hesitate to go to the health center, and after some testing, I was told me that it wasn't rheumatoid arthritis, so it was likely some form of arthritis, and probably not serious. They tried a couple of medications that they didn't think was going to help, but they figured it was worth a try, and of course they didn't help.

After some more testing, I saw the doctor again, and the verdict was not only was I healthy, it would be inaccurate to say that I was as as healthy as a horse, but that a horse would be so lucky to be as healthy as I am. Armed with that information, he told me that if I lost some significant weight, even though I was well within what could be considered to be not overweight, that reducing the stress on my joints might allow them to heal on their own.

With my spirit severely depressed, it was no longer easy to see Nunavut in only a positive light, and I began to notice more of what was happening around me. As I became more determined to eat healthier, I began to realize, that though the Co-op and Northern stores were subsidized, I had to shop carefully, as a fairly significant portion of the food they were selling to us was expired, frost damaged (even in the summer), spoiled or downright rotten.

I found myself buying very little dry goods locally, as even with outright exorbitant shipping costs, buying goods on eBay and via mail order, goods shipped directly to my doorstep, even coming all the way from China, cost a fraction of the price of what local retailers were charging. Having a MasterCard, I have always had the option of buying goods on-line, enjoying the financial protection my credit card offered. Most Inuit, however, do not have access to credit cards, and have no choice but to pay whatever the local retailers charge, and only have available very poor quality merchandise, for truly insane prices.

Making the situation even worse, the government is discontinuing the food mail program, completely removing the Inuit people's only source of decent quality food.

Despite it's exorbitant cost and the capability to be as fast as any other high speed Internet offerings available in North America, Netkaster continues to be not much faster than dial-up, and I have discontinued my service from them, unable to justify the outrageous cost. I have yet to get phone service, whether land-line or cell, again, as I am unable to justify the exorbitant (despite being subsidized) cost.

Early this winter, the garage in my bosses duplex in which I was living burnt down, and I found myself homeless. At that time I found that the housing situation wasn't any better.

Though the federal government had made a firm commitment via the Nunavut Land Claims Agreement to afford the Inuit people economical and affordable housing, and enable them to acquire such, the actual situation was that subsidized housing was only available to those who did not work, no subsidies provided to anyone working, and additional housing allowances only given to government workers, most of whom are not local people.

To this day, I still see government jobs being given to non-locals, even when qualified Inuit have applied for the jobs in question, and not too uncommonly, given to unqualified individuals (sometimes Inuit or usually non-local people). The only training positions I have yet too see become available are in Renewable Resources, a field where many Inuit require little, if any training.

A small portion of Inuit work for the government, enjoying access to some of the only decent housing in the community, but when they cease working for the government, they are thrown out, and usually move away from the community, no longer having access to affordable housing.

I get angry and frustrated, but once an Inuk knows what it means to not live in poverty, I understand that they don't want to stay and willingly submit themselves to such complete and total poverty.

Though various programs such as programs to assist Inuit to purchase materials to build a house, or assist in purchasing a house, or to assist in renovating a house, only a handful of people have even benefited from the program. Additionally the

Material Assistance Program has already been discontinued (and I had just qualified too), and rumors are that the other programs will follow suit.

It was not fun packing up my stuff, building more crates (which are sitting on the land) in which to put my stuff that would not fit in the old trailer I already had a significant portion of my property.

I am now homeless, forced to rely on the kindness of my relatives to take me in, because even though I earn around fifty thousand a year, the cost of available housing, the cost of utilities, and the cost to feed oneself exceeds my take home income. If my ultimate goal wasn't to create a better life for myself and others in Nunavut, at this point in time I would be better off to quit my job and go on welfare, just so I could have a home, or move away abandoning everything I have been working for.

I don't even have an option to share a home with a roommate, because the housing corporation charges rent based on income, so I can not even acquire affordable housing by pooling my resources with someone else.

To add to all that, the government has reversed it's commitment to increase employment of local tradesman halving the required Inuit content and slowly eliminating it's use of local contractors.

To top all that, the GN, despite the governments commitment to increase availability of education for the Inuit people, continue to place barriers to education that do not exist anywhere else in Canada.

The largest barrier that exists in Nunavut is the fact that the Inuit CANNOT borrow money to go to school. I have been down that road before, and because the GN has made a commitment to provide funding for the Inuit people, borrowing money to go to school is only available in extreme cases, and only then one has a better chance of winning the lottery then to get approved.

The second barrier to education is the fact that the GN limits the institutions the Inuit may attend, and limits the funding available to the Inuit, so that many programs, especially those that cost more, are not available to the Inuit. Unless an Inuk or his/her family has enough money, going to school at the more expensive and usually higher quality institutions, is next to impossible, so that the higher quality educational institutions are just not available to the Inuit people.

Anywhere else in Canada, even if an individual has to borrow money, Canadians have full access to higher education.

As an Inuk, who wasn't raised in Nunavut, I have already known how the Government restricts access to education available to all other Canadians (an Inuk not from Nunavut cannot get funding from Nunavut, and cannot borrow money to go to school), and being exposed to other areas of the country, I have seen how education is denied to the Inuit people.

Knowing this, I still wasn't concerned about going to school for my apprenticeship, simply because as an apprentice, I would qualify for employment insurance, and that would be enough to allow me to pay my bills, and to live on while at school for the two months of school required each year.

To be certain, I confirmed that the department of education would be paying for my travel costs ahead of time, and that the school would be billing them for tuition directly. I was only required to pay dorm costs, books and school supplies costs, and my cost of living, and even then they would be giving supplementary allowances to cover books, supplies, and supplement my living costs, all of which both the GN and EI confirmed to me would be received in addition to my EI.

Once again, the reality of the situation has turned out quite different than the GN has made it seem to be.

After signing up to be an apprentice, working for around a year and a half, and accumulating nearly enough hours for first and second year carpentry, I had to contact them and inquire if they were ever going to send me to school. I am finally going to school, almost two years after signing up for my apprenticeship, and I have now gained first hand knowledge of how the GN is deliberately stopping the Inuit from becoming tradesmen. I had already been wondering why many Inuit I know of who had begun their apprenticeships had never finished.

As it turns out, even though on paper it seems that with all the money the GN and EI were supposedly going to be giving me, I would be making out like a bandit. What has actually happened, I can only define as outright cruelty. Though, apparently I was qualified for a significant sum of money from the GN, the amount of which would be the maximum I might be able to receive, I only actually received a small portion of the sum I was eligible for.

Even worse, EI did not give me any money for the first week

after I was done working before school (no explanation), and reduced my benefits for vacation pay, two weeks waiting period, and receiving supplementary income from the GN, such that it appears that I am only going to be receiving three weeks of benefits while attending an eight week course.

Simply asking the other apprentices in my class who have been getting their benefits, going to school in the Northwest Territories, I have confirmed that it appears that the apprentices in the NWT are getting their full eight weeks of benefits.

Adding up the numbers, it appears that I will be receiving less money than the NWT apprentices, who have a significantly lower cost of living, money in which I would need to pay for books, school supplies, my cost of living in my community, and my cost of living at school.

Ironically, since I am currently homeless, I don't have a cost of living in my community, and financially I am just going to make it, though a good portion of the first few paychecks when I start working again will be going to catch up and pay back the money I borrowed from my boss to help pay my cost of living while going to school.

Tragically, since I doubt that I will still be homeless when I go for my next year of school (I am working towards not being homeless after all), I am not going to be able to afford to be able to go to school, and the likelihood that my employment will continue afterward is highly doubtful, because as the subsidies my employer receives for an apprentice ceases, and due to my joint pain, there are others who cost less, will work significantly longer hours, and do not need to be employed on a permanent full time basis.

I am definitely not going to be able to rely on the government to help me return to a mode of life to be able to sustain myself on the land, as the very few snowmobiles, quads, boats, and various hunting gear are rarely brought up to the community, and only then they are usually raffled off by lottery because of the huge demand. Quite literally, the local Co-op has raffled of more vehicles and hunting gear, simply as part of doing business in the community. The amount of vehicles and hunting gear brought into the community by the government does not even make up much more of a small portion of all the money, vehicles and hunting gear raffled off or given away in the typical community events, social gatherings or activities typical of most communities.

Looking back on before I came to Nunavut, from nothing I earned myself a good trade, working and earning enough experience and a good enough reputation to have a fair selection of work within the trade, whether within management or working at the trade itself, I was earning fairly decent earnings, I had found affordable housing, I had a good reliable vehicle, I could afford to pay my living costs and have a decent amount of spending money.

Since moving to Nunavut, I make more money than I ever have, but I don't have a home, there isn't any affordable housing available to me, the only vehicles I have is a quad I am fixing up that I got off my cousin whose husband assembled from spare parts and a snowmobile I am assembling from spare parts, I don't have any spending money, in the short term I may no longer be employed in my chosen trade anymore, and my stuff is subject to a significant amount of theft and vandalism because I am considered "rich" due to having a job.

As I live in complete and total poverty, despite being a positively contributing member of society, I can't help feel a strong and utter sense of betrayal from the government who is supposed to be working to bring the Inuit people out of the dark ages.

The federal government even goes so far as to say that it has to "give" the GN over a billion dollars a year just to operate, inferring that the Inuit people are a huge drain and cost to the Canadian taxpayer, angering the population against the Inuit people, completely ignoring and obfuscating the facts that the federal government's income from Nunavut exceeds the money they are putting into Nunavut.

The sense of betrayal I experience deepens significantly when you consider that under the Nunavut Land Claims Agreement the federal government has made commitments that are above and beyond moneys it earns in Nunavut to provide health care, education, affordable housing and the reduction of poverty in Nunavut, and the have yet to put any more money into Nunavut than what they are already taking out of Nunavut.

Not only is the federal government not providing the services it agreed to the Inuit people, it is systematically removing and discontinuing the marginal programs that were already in place to try to address the Inuit peoples needs.

Difficult as it is, I had already made something of myself before I came to Nunavut, and knowing what to do, I can do it again. If I must, I will sacrifice and live in complete poverty if it means I can work towards improving my lot in life.

Through my personal experience, I can say with certainty, in my particular case, Canada has denied me medical care, education, affordable housing and protection from poverty, in complete and total breach of the Nunavut Land Claims Agreement and all other relevant contracts between Canada and it's indigenous peoples.

It is not all that surprising that NTI (Nunavut Tungavik Incorporated) are trying to hold Canada accountable for breaching it's agreements, but it's also not too surprising that NTI's only source of remedy, is through the very courts who will always rule in favor of the interests (Canada's) it is tasked to protect.

I am writing this to give voice to what I have experienced, in the hopes that someday my voice will be recognized and heard. I am sending a copy to the GN and Canada, to remind them that they are in breach of the Nunavut Land Claims Agreement, and give them a chance to remedy the situation.

Unfortunately, nothing I have written here, even being my first hand knowledge, isn't anything that is new or unknown in Canada, so I hope what I have written has been written well enough to get people to notice events that have been largely ignored for the most part.

Hopefully, with some hard work and determination, I hope I can restore the nightmare I have been enveloped in, back into a dream, but it looks like Canada will have little to do in making that a reality.

As I finish this letter, I would like to remind everyone that, almost universally, the Inuit I know living in these conditions, do not wish to live in poverty. Everyone, not just the Inuit, want access to education and health care, affordable housing, decent and affordable food, protection from poverty and crime, and freedom to pursue typical traditional activities.

Unlike most other Inuit, I know the rest of Canada has complete access to all these things, and when these things have been denied to the Inuit people, and when Canada has promised all of the aforementioned in exchange for the Inuit people's surrender of all land rights to some of the largest and richest areas of Canada, denying these things to the Inuit people is not only not fair, it is outright wanton cruelty.

Give me, or any other Inuk, access to education and health care, affordable housing, decent and affordable food, protection from poverty and crime, and freedom to pursue typical traditional activities, and I will free myself from poverty. Deny me these things, and unlike most other Inuit, I still have the capability and experience, having already learned how to do so, to free myself from poverty, but I will suffer greatly.

I don't need a handout, and neither do the Inuit people, when all we have only ever asked for is the rights and services our tax dollar affords us, and we have already signed over our people's land rights for the same rights and services all other Canadians enjoy, when the Inuit could have asked for so much more.

When a people signs over everything they have, just to be treated fairly, you begin to understand how desperate they were.

So I ask you; are you truly this cruel and vicious as well, or are you going to add your voice to mine, and ask Canada; WHAT THE HELL!!!

Chapter 10 – Lonely

Right now, as I lay in bed, I am feeling so lonely, my heart aches.

However, despite my confusion and slight homophobia, today I now know what my sexual orientation is, because I am wishing I had a man to hold and embrace me while we lay in bed, to tell me he loves me, to tell me about his day, to regale him with the events of my day, to make me feel sexy and beautiful, and to make love to me the way a man makes love to a woman.

I am desperately wishing the day that I will begin to be seen as a woman, desirable and beautiful, would arrive sooner. I find myself cold and lonely, and I start to find the idea of a man to snuggle up to as more and more appealing each and every day that passes.

As I lose weight, and as I notice my strength fading over time, and though I am a little alarmed by how the lack of manly strength makes me feel very vulnerable, I can appreciate how my body is slowly approaching the female norm in size, and I can start to see that I could become a beautiful, desirable woman.

I am not exactly sure why I am starting to find men appealing in a sexual way, and honestly though I find the prospect a little frightening, I find some peace of mind that I am becoming able to sexually desire someone, and it makes the lonely heartache a little easier to bear.

At times now, I start to find myself wondering what I will find attractive in a man. I wonder if I will start to appreciate the good looks of handsome men and become turned on by their appearance, or will I be attracted to the strength of their character.

I know with certainty that I desire someone who loves and respects me, and has the strength of character to challenge me intellectually and emotionally when needed.

I now find that I have an intense desire to dress in the clothing of my wanted gender all the time, but I also have an even greater desire to be sexually appealing, to the point that I feel strongly pained for not looking like a woman. I find in myself a powerful need to be sexually desirable to men, that conflicts greatly with my appearance.

I don't think it is unhealthy to want to be beautiful, but unlike genetic women, I don't have a lifetime of experience learning to deal with that emotion, and I am also unsure of what is reasonable for me to expect to be able to accomplish appearance wise.

I have an overwhelming desire to figure out what I want in a man, but I feel like I am trying to pull something out of myself that has yet to define itself, and I wish I could because then if the man who was to be my better half were reading my journal writings, I fantasize he would think to himself; "Wow! She has such a beautiful spirit, and hey, I am exactly the kind of guy she is looking for!"

I know that is pretty unlikely, especially if I can not put into words what I would find attractive in a man, but I can't help but fantasize that my prince charming is out there, just waiting to scoop me off my feet, and make my heart whole.

In hindsight, I suppose my heart has been telling me I have desired my own prince charming my whole life, but like other feelings, I have been suppressing that heartache for a long time.

On a positive note, if a man does come to desire me, and he can get past the fact that I was born a man, than I know then there is a greater chance he actually has true feelings of love for me.

Chapter 11 – A New Being

This morning, I watched Tron Legacy, and it broke me up and tore apart my emotions like no movie ever has ever done to me before.

At first I had no idea why it was affecting me so strongly until Quorra asked Sam what the Sun was like, and I immediately understood why.

She had never seen the Sun, because she never existed in our world before.

It was likely she never experienced it's warmth, it's radiance, it's sheer beauty, and then my heart painfully ached for a beautiful sunny day, that I might bask in it's warmth, to see it once more with all it's splendor and all the magnificence it reveals throughout nature and our universe.

The emotions hit me, harder than if I had been hit by a freight train, and despite the harshness of the weather in Kugluktuk today, or maybe because of it, I suddenly appreciated how wonderful our world can be, as if I had never been alive when I experienced everything before now.

It feels like the emotions I never had when I saw the world in a sort of detached appreciation overcame me all at once, like an emotional flood, and I could not help but cry.

As painful as the sudden influx of emotion was, I can not deny how wonderful the pain is, that sudden emotional response, to experiences that, though I had an inherent appreciation already, had at this singular point in time, become so beautiful.

It was as an epiphany, to see why people have such a strong response to a wonderful, sunny day. To know what others feel when they bask in the warmth of the Sun, to understand how great it feels to walk barefoot through the warm sand, to really feel what it means to run my hands through the warm sand.

The emotions fade, and the emotional changes within me become apparent. I won't ever see the world the same way again as I see how emotions completely change how I view everything, and the next time I get to go to a beach on a warm sunny day, I hope I don't break down and cry.

If I do, I won't be embarrassed or try to hold the emotions back, because I don't ever want to hold anything back again.

As I watched Tron Legacy, I did not care about any of the characters except Quorra, who had such a quiet want to experience the wonder and beauty of our world, and I found that portion of me who was Vanida Corazon Kemaktun Plamondon identified with her so strongly, it was somewhat painful.

Odd as it may seem, I could also empathize with the plight of Clu at the end of the movie.

In the beginning of the year 2010, Vanida broke through every barrier I had created to lock her away forever, born a new being to this world. It was as though the story of Kevin Flynn, Clu, and Quorra was my story.

It was as if I had created my own Clu, whom I had become, completely locking myself away, trapping myself within, but within, trapped with me, Vanida was born and came into being. When she broke free, the only way I was able to save her and protect her, was to reintegrate my own Clu back into myself, destroying both of us, leaving only Vanida.

Like Clu, my own creation fought fervently to protect itself, and the way Clu re-purposed Tron to fight his battles, my creation used my fears, anger and emotion to protect itself, until my emotions remembered and began to serve my own being, to protect me, to protect me.

Vanida is a new being, she sees the world as one who has not seen it before, and marvels at it's beauty. She is curious and inquisitive, like a child, because she is, emotionally, very young.

Unlike her predecessor, she doesn't shield herself from the pain and anguish she may feel from others who may wish to inflict such on her, nor does she wish to. Knowing what may come is the only way for her to prepare herself for that pain, so she marvels and appreciates the wisdom and experience of her elders, including the one who was before her.

She is actually fearful and afraid of what lies before her, but she also marvels at the courage she can draw upon to face those fears, emotions that were were not present in any appreciable degree in her predecessor.

Understand that she is terrified and afraid to lose her new found self, that her predecessor might come back and try to lock her away again, and she fights with every ounce of her being to understand what she is feeling, to welcome it completely, unwilling to suppress any emotion, scared beyond reason that she might return to being that detached, self destructive being she had used to be.

She strongly dislikes being told that she cannot have her hearts desire, and feels tremendous pain at the prospect that she may not attain all that she hopes and desires, that she might be deprived of attaining any of her dreams.

Like most other young people, she isn't ready or prepared, but she can't help but forging ahead fervently, unwilling to hold herself back, fearful of the consequences, hoping beyond all hope to not make any catastrophic mistakes.

Her limitations or capabilities are not known to her, she only knows that our world will continue to place it's limits upon her, and that the Creator will make her capable of anything the Creator would want of her.

Her heart aches and longs for many blessings from the Creator, hoping that as she continues to cultivate, protect and her respect her existing gifts, she will be granted more and more of her hearts desire.

Finally, she want to proclaim from the highest mountain who she is, for all the world to see, but she is afraid for herself and her loved ones of the possible hate and ignorance that might be directed at her or those she loves.

I am her, I have stopped being who I had been for some time, and she has liberated me, and she has truly made me free. To become her was to become my true self, and only my doubts from who I had been remain, to test and strengthen my resolve.

It pains me that the prescribed path to ones sex change is a cruel and possibly unforgiven process, that I must dress and act as a member of the desired sex whilst still looking like that of the former sex, for a long time before treatment starts, but I am preparing for that as best I can.

Chapter 12 – Fingernails

This morning, I decided to give myself a manicure, though I did not exactly know how. I was kind of getting fed up with my nails looking so harsh and ugly.

Of course, when I was done, I started wondering how my nails would look with a coat of nail polish, and eventually I could not resist and I painted my fingernails. I was quite happy with how the nails on my left hand turned out, and though the nails on my right hand did not come out as well (it was more difficult to do my right hand because of my right handedness), I thought they turned out all right.

After spending all morning on my nails, however, I realized that after doing all that work, I did not want to remove the nail polish, and I doubted that I could wear gloves to hide them all the time.

Thinking about my choices in the matter, I found I had only a few choices available to me, remove the nail polish, hide my fingers, let people wonder why I had painted fingernails, or reevaluate when I was planning to reveal to the community of my desire to become a woman.

Originally, I had been planning on reaching a goal weight and finish permanent hair removal of my facial hair before revealing to the community my dual sexuality and begin my transition to womanhood by beginning to dress and live as a woman.

As it often happens in life, events in my life have been forcing me to reevaluate my plans.

First of all, I have recently begun taking a female health

supplement which is definitely causing my body hair to slow it's growth considerably and become somewhat finer, and unless I am imagining things, I am starting to grow breasts.

I had been noticing for the last few days a slight jiggle in my chest, which for someone who has never experienced such a sensation, stood out as an unusual feeling that seemed a little out of place. At first, I just discounted the feeling as one in which I had never noticed before.

Additionally, for the last week, partly because I am not working right now, I have been wearing woman's clothes full time, only covering up with wearing jeans and a jacket over top when working outside or going out.

I had found recently, that as time passes, I have begun to slowly replace much of my learned masculine behavior with feminine behavior as I learn feminine habit, and as I open myself up to acting according to my emotional state without concern for appearing masculine.

As an example, I have found myself sitting with my knees together as much as possible, horror and shame overcoming me when I forget with the realization that, had I been wearing a skirt or dress, I could have been revealing my underwear to the world in my moment of forgetfulness.

On the computer, I type differently, compensating for the long fingernails, that for the past year, I only trim when the nails break and become damaged. Even though I do not wish to conform to female stereotypes, despite wanting to be female, it does in fact bother me when I break a nail. I even take my time while working, more than I ever have, just for the simple fact that I don't want to damage my nails.

Since last fall, I do not ever exert myself to the maximum extant my strength allows, as I have learned that maximum exertion leads to building or maintaining muscle mass, and I want muscles even less than I want a hole in the head.

As I lose body mass, and I treat my body, permanently removing hair a little bit at a time, I come closer to my goals, and as I come closer and closer a small bit at a time towards looking female, I want to be a woman more than ever. At times I have become so desperate, I have come very close to tears, and my heart aches painfully at the possibility.

At a certain point it become harder and harder to hide what I want, as I want to hide it less and less as time passes. I suppose I could keep hiding, but eventually that becomes unrealistic.

The worst feeling I experience because I am hiding what I want, is the fact that I feel like I am lying to all my friends and family I know and love, and that fraudulent feeling gnaws away and fills me with shame and doubt.

The only reasonable course of action left to me for my peace of mind is that I am going to have to reveal to my friends and family what I am going through, and hope for the best.

Once again I have to face my fear, paranoia and doubt, and hope for understanding. I have no doubt that I will have to face fear, ignorance and hatred in the community, but my hope is that my writing of what I am going through will continue to help friends and family understand what I am going through, and know what I am undergoing is not easy or without careful consideration of my possible choices.

Chapter 13 – Becoming Myself

Since my last entry in this journal, I have started to distribute to my family copies of this journal, been to see a psychiatrist's office for their initial assessment for my treatment, and I have begun to publicly live and dress as a woman.

In many ways, since my last entry, I have been experiencing strong emotional turmoil as I have begun to share with my family what I am doing and what I am going through in the meantime.

I had also been agonizing considerably over how I was going to come out to the community as a whole about my transgenderism.

After my last entry, I decided I could not wait anymore, and though I was not happy with where I was with my weight loss and permanent hair removal, I was experiencing more and more feelings of 'desperate need to become a woman' (for a lack of a better description).

Essentially, as I came closer and closer to my goals, and as I have come to see and actually believe I could become a woman, but not just a woman, but a beautiful woman, I was becoming more and more desperate.

There had been many nights recently, where I have been curled up in a ball as I lay in waiting to fall asleep, in deep emotional pain almost ready to break out in tears, as I wanted to be a woman more and more until it was beginning to become a very painful need and desire.

I was also starting to wonder if, that when I started to live and dress as a woman if I was going to become a complete emotional wreck as that powerful need to become a woman consumed me, and I found that prospect quite frightening.

Anyway, as I was packing my bag for my trip to see the psychiatrist specializing in gender identity disorders for the first time, I just could not bring myself to pack any of my men's clothes.

I knew at that point in time, as I was in the process of revealing my transgenderism to the rest of my family, there really was not any possibility that I was going to go back to wearing what I considered ugly clothing, and I was going to wear only woman's clothes once I got to the city and I was going to have to give serious thought on how I was going to reveal to the community as a whole about myself.

For the time being, I put on a woman's shirt, men's jeans and covered up with my jacket and a pair of gloves to cover up. I really did not want to cover up and hide my clothing and for the entire trip to the city I was a complete emotional wreck as I struggled with my desire to show to the world who I am, and fear of people's reactions driving me to hide my woman's clothes.

It truly, really did not help that I had just seen a preview of the new Green Lantern movie and I realized Ryan Reynolds was smoking hot, so now I was struggling with not just the fact that I was beginning to become attracted to men, I was already starting to find particular men attractive.

So there I was, on the way to the city, wanting desperately to show to the world who I am, terrified of what the evil ones of our society might want to do to me if I came across them, lusting after Ryan Reynolds and hornier than I have ever been since the first time I got so horny that I thought I could lose control of myself.

Needless to say, the flight to the city was a very uncomfortable, marginally traumatic experience, and when the flight landed in the city, I had never been so relieved in my life.

I guess I was so relieved, I understood then what an emotional burden it was to hide and cover myself up, and I knew then I was going through some unnecessary pain by doing so and I needed to face the fear I was going through.

When I found the Larga Homes driver, loaded my bag in their van and got in, I unzipped my jacket as it was too warm to leave my jacket zipped, and I took off my gloves.

Their were a few momentary odd glances as the other passengers got in the van, but no one actually paid me any attention and my heart soared as I began to really feel the freedom to be myself for the first time in my life.

The trip was rather uneventful on the way into the city from the airport, and I was left alone to ponder my thoughts in peace and I really felt a warm glow of peace and happiness permeate my body in a way I haven't experienced in a long time.

To my complete and utter surprise, that desperate desire and need to become a woman was completely gone, and I was somewhat confused by that change in my emotions, though I knew I still wanted to be a woman, I just did not know at the time why that desperation suddenly disappeared.

We arrived at the boarding home, and the staff sorted us out, giving us rooms, giving us the home's rules and telling us of it's amenities.

I went to my assigned room, and when I went inside I saw two single beds, and someone else's stuff in the room, I realized that the health center had not informed the boarding home of what I was in the city for treatment for, and I had not considered the possibility that the boarding home would be shared rooms, and had not made sure the health center had passed along the relevant information to the boarding home.

Considering how vulnerable I was feeling at this time, I really did not want to room with a man, and though I really never had seen myself as a man for most of my life, I did see just then that I never had a mental picture of myself as a man, and I was already developing a female mental self portrait.

I had to calm myself, and remind myself that I have shared a room with men before, and because of my masculine appearance I was also very unlikely to be molested, as it was unlikely that I was physically appealing in a feminine way anyway.

So I steeled myself for what was to come, my self confidence nearly destroyed already, and I set out to get ready to go do my shopping, as there was a ton of stuff I needed and wanted to get while in the city.

My roommate returned just prior to me going to shower and I introduced myself and he introduced himself, and I checked with him if he was going to bothered with rooming with someone who wanted to be a woman, and he said he didn't care, so when he left I showered and continued getting ready for my first shopping trip as a woman.

I had yet to get any woman's jeans, since it just was not possible to figure out what jeans will fit me without trying them on, so I put on a pair of jean printed leggings and a really pretty shirt I liked. I got my jacket and sneakers on and I headed out to Walmart as the first stop on my expedition.

I was just crossing the street, literally only a block away from Larga, when I walked passed a couple crossing the street the other way. The woman looked away from the man she was apparently talking to and looked at myself, laughed out loud and continued on her way.

I think I kind of staggered as I finished crossing the street, and I almost broke down to cry on the spot. I don't know if she had been trying to be cruel, but it felt like she had stabbed me in the heart with a red hot iron.

I numbly kept walking to find a cash machine at the mall across the two streets in front of Larga, and I suddenly felt hideous and very self conscious.

By the time I had found a cash machine, I was all right again as I forced myself to remember that I did not care what a perfect stranger thought, and though I was somewhat choked up, I got over the hurt very quickly.

I was feeling much better by the time I got some change for the bus, and was heading downtown to catch a train to a shopping area where there was an Walmart easily accessible by public transportation. I began to feel really hurt again by the time the bus got downtown as the bus filled up but the seats right around me emptied out.

Even though I try not to care what strangers think, it still hurt a lot.

My nerves were totally shot when I was heading to catch the train, and I saw a handful of train cops at the entrance to the proof of payment area, and as I was passing them, one of them turned to me and gruffly demanded I show my transfer.

I let out a kind of choked "eee" in surprise and fear as I suddenly noticed he was a really big guy, and I got really frightened when I saw he was probably capable of really physically hurting me.

As I scrambled to get my transfer out, I saw the look of guilt and confusion cross his face at my fear, and it was pretty easy to figure out he did not mean to scare me, but it was too late and I had honestly become scared.

As far as I can remember, this was the first time in my life I actually trembled in fear, and I was totally shocked that things that did not even faze me before, could so easily take me by surprise and terrify me so completely.

It then occurred to me that it was probably a really poor idea for a woman to be wandering the city by herself, and I was one of the transgendered, a group with a known hostility, hatred and ignorance oftentimes directed at them.

I missed the first train, as I sat at the train platform's seating, rooted in fear, like a deer in the path of headlights, scared, wanting to go home and hide, just all around afraid.

I found a deep well of courage I did not know existed, and I remembered that the people who had just scared me witless, the train cops, were also there for our protection. I found deep relief as it occurred to me I was using public transportation at a busy time in the evening and there would be no shortage of people around and I really was not in much danger.

I would have laughed at how silly I was being, if only I had the conviction of how silly I was being, to match my unexpected courage.

It's a good thing that my mom and many others have often told me that it's okay to have bad feelings, it only matters what you do with those feelings that matters, so that I knew at least that it was all right for me to be afraid, I just had to face the fear.

It was not exactly easy, but I knew if I did not overcome the fear, I would not be able to pick up the stuff I needed or wanted, and I prayed for the Creator to keep me safe.

I made it to Walmart, and though I was suffering from a lack of confidence, and very shaken self esteem, I got my shopping done.

I bought a few pairs of jeans that were comfy and fit me fairly well, and I was almost elated to find, that even though I already knew men's jeans were already not fitting me very well, woman's low-rise jeans actually fit me nicely.

I also saw a really nice denim purse I thought looked cool, and a really cool denim hat with a simple white shoelace style bow, and when I saw the hat, I knew it was for me, since I knew for me I was probably be a blue jeans type of woman most of the time anyway, and I really liked the purse and I figured if I am going to be living as a woman, I might as well see if I would rather have a purse than a wallet.

Finally, I was finished not long before Walmart closed, and as I was outside in the parking lot packing my purchases into the medium sized wheeled plastic box, I realized it was now late and there would be very few people about, and just as few on public transportation, and all my earlier fears returned.

I put on a pair of new jeans I bought, and being less self conscious really helped out.

I was really scared to go home by myself, and I really prayed to the Creator for protection.

Halfway to the train station from Walmart, one of the wheels on my luggage case broke, and I started to cry and sniffle a little bit, and I did not really know what I was going to do, since I couldn't replace the wheel now that Walmart was closed for the day.

Not knowing what else to do, I decided to lift the box on my shoulder to see if I could handle carrying the weight short distances. I was really surprised to find out I was completely freaked out about bringing home a load in which, as it turns out, I could easily carry.

I started to laugh, nearly dropping my stuff, as I also remember I was moving and dragging around appliances by myself the day before, and I found myself feeling so ridiculous and silly for being so frightened when I am so far from being helpless.

Sure maybe my strength isn't very much compared to a big strong man, but I at least have some basic self defense capabilities, and I know I would have an excellent chance of escaping most bad situations as long as I am not too proud to run away.

I sure had a good trip home that evening when I stopped being scared, and I even started to pretend that people who were staring at me were looking at me because I had a hot, sexy body and I got most of my self confidence back.

When I got back to my room, I found my roommate was gone and I now had the room to myself. I was started to feel good about myself, and I then quickly did my nails (not very well as I rushed them, mind you) and I went to bed face down, arms hanging down over the sides so hopefully my nail polish could survive the night.

Despite the serious awkwardness of the sleeping position, I was so tired and emotionally drained, I quickly passed out. The nails survived the night, but were somewhat less than spectacular for the abuse.

I got dressed, put my wallet and basic essentials in my purse, put my hat on, and went to the kitchen to go get breakfast.

It felt like my new hat was a knights helmet, my purse a shield, my new pants and the shirt I put on to go with it was armor, and my freshly painted nails was my sword. Despite the emotional difficulty of the previous day, I now had all the courage I needed in order to be myself in public.

That day was really great, I got my ears pierced, I went to Lenscrafters and I bought cool new glasses, though they would have to mail them out to me once they got authorization for payment from Federal health care.

When I was arrived for my first appointment for treatment of my transgenderism, I found four people waiting for me, and I was so overwhelmed suddenly, I immediately wanted to turn around and run away.

Turns out, in addition to the doctor"s intern who was going to interview me, there was a psychiatric nurse, a transgender PHD Candidate, and another doctor who wanted to sit in on the interview.

At first I was quite intimidated, but not long after I found I really liked the attention. The interviewer had me quickly go over my story and why I wanted to be a woman. He asked questions and sought clarification in a fairly straightforward manner, and I very quickly became comfortable, and it seems like the interview flew by.

Afterward, he went to review with the Doctor and I socialized for a bit with the others which finally relaxed me.

The doctor came and talked with me next, and he went over filling in the details of treatment I did not know, gave me a prescription for male hormone blockers, extra literature for me to read and to also pass on to the health care center in my home community and a carry letter (a letter from him explaining the transition I will be undergoing, that would help me from getting in trouble from things like using the woman's washroom), and told me the things I did not know about transitioning from male to female.

He scheduled me for an appointment in January, and told me

that if I was ready then, I would start female hormones next.

Honestly, my visit to begin my transition to womanhood was the most wonderful experience I have had seeing any type of mental health professional.

It truly felt like their approach was simply; What do you want? Are you certain? How can we be of service? When you are ready and fulfill the requirements of the process we will move you on the next step.

After that appointment I still had some shopping and a few things left to do, but I had completely gained all my self confidence back, and I felt like a superwoman, so needless to say the rest of the day was pretty nice.

With all I had to do while in the city, I had not actually had a chance to think about how I was going to reveal my transgenderism to the community until I was sitting on the plane, just a few minutes from home.

I decided it really was not a big deal for me to just live and dress as a woman and my unusual appearance would indicate that something's up, and if they were truly interested I would tell them anything they know, and most probably not even care and probably would not even react in any negative way.

I stepped off the plane ready to become a new woman, but more important than anything else, I was ready for the most wonderful thing in the world, to be myself.

Chapter 14 – Not Prepared For Changes

Too be honest, I was expecting changes in my body, but as I was only on a male hormone blocker, I did not actually expect much changes, and I was wrong.

Of course, the women in my family have told me, and are now emphasizing, that it is harder to be a woman, than it is to be a man. I already believed them, but it has been something else to begin experiencing those difficulties first hand.

First of all, from what I have begun to experience so far, it is definitely easier to be a man, than it is to be a woman, and it does not seem to have much to do with peeing standing up.

Long before I began the male hormone blockers, as I began to embrace, explore and reveal my emotions, starting to become an emotional creature, I had already started to experience change.

As I began to open myself up to my feelings and also slowly begun to reveal them to others, to eventually reveal them to the whole world, I began to experience a very frightening, quite scary sense of vulnerability at the prospect of exposing my weaknesses to the world.

To say that I was terrified at times, would be putting it mildly, as I feared that my vulnerability would be used to really hurt me scared me a lot.

Every time I revealed my vulnerabilities to the world, however, the Creator gave me a well of strength to draw upon, until I began to learn that by sharing my emotions, dreams and hopes did not make me vulnerable, but make me stronger.

Recently, I found that I could not think of anything anyone could hurt me with emotionally, because I had run out of things I was hiding and suppressing, and I would rather be shot than to hide or suppress anything else again.

I can not say I am not afraid of anything now, because so much scares me that never scared me before, but I seem to have no shortage of courage to draw upon to face those fears.

Also, for some time now, as I have been losing significant weight, and accordingly, significant muscle mass. I have been becoming physically weaker and much less capable physically.

Last weekend, as I had already been on male hormone blockers for just a little under a week, I noticed another significant change. Though it did not seem that I had exerted myself too much that day, I overdid it and ended up in significant muscle pain throughout my body.

I was also a little cranky and unhappy as I also discovered that no testosterone meant muscle pain was significantly more painful than before.

Telling my cousins and aunts just got me a cheerful response of "Now you know how we feel."

I also had a not so much fun episode opening a pickle jar where I ended up screaming at the jar; "Quit stereotyping me cuz I want to be a woman, YOU PIECE OF S#!T !!!" which I am pretty sure those are the words I used.

When I calmed down, I used a knife to pry the lid to break the vacuum, and the jar opened easily.

It really bothered me because I freaked out on the jar, as their were a couple of jars I have had much trouble opening when I was significantly stronger, and I had to tell myself that as I am less physically capable I need to use my brain more and stop acting like a dumb man.

It also felt so good to be able to say to someone, "men are so dumb" and the usual response has been "You only figured that out now?" and of course I have to point out that, no I have known for some time, but I have been holding it in.

Another significant change I have noticed recently, has been the fact I have been becoming all over the place emotionally during the day. Sometimes I have been getting so cheerful, I have felt perky and bouncy, and I have caught myself bouncing on my toes, and sometimes I just want to curl up in a ball and pout.

The moods swings are not very serious, but I really love the perky, bubbly feeling, because it feels so fun, and sometimes I want to dance, which also feels really fun. It's been so long since I have felt so good, it also makes me feel all warm and glowy in my heart sometimes.

I won't go over the emotional changes, like starting to become attracted to men, that I have covered in previous entries, but they continue to surprise me, even though they are not that new of a feeling because I can't help marvel at how normal the feelings seem to be to have.

I also notice, that now that I have stopped hiding, and begun to just be myself, the emotions that used to be so painful, seem so trivial now, telling me the only reason I had hurt so much, was simply because I was not being true to myself.

The last few changes I noticed I really, really love. For one, I find that daily feeling of tiredness and total lack of motivation at the end of the day, pretty much gone.

If I don't hurt myself, I can pretty much keep busy all day, as long as I take frequent breaks, keep my fluids up, and eat when I am hungry. That's good, since I am not capable of as much now, so I guess it balances out somewhat.

Even though I haven't changed very much, I still did not know what to expect, and I am as apprehensive about starting female hormones as much as I am looking forward to it.

Chapter 15 - Sexual Frustration

Honestly, one thing I really, really did not expect, was how sexually frustrated I was going to become.

Before I started on the spironolactone (a male hormone blocker) I was constantly, physically approaching the edge of arousal, so much so, just the wind blowing the right way could make me horny. I really hated that, but I could masturbate and it would relieve me somewhat.

Now, I don't become physically aroused very much, but emotionally I am constantly feeling a strong desire to be held, to kiss, to touch, to be touched, to be wanted sexually, and to be loved.

I have been trying to relieve those feelings by masturbating, but it just seems to be a fruitless endeavor except when I am also horny at the time.

I can't seem to stay focused, and I get distracted, and I just seem to get more frustrated in the end.

There are a couple of movie stars I have started to notice and become attracted to, and I try fantasizing about them, but it really does not seem to help to fantasize.

Before, all I really had to do to relieve built up sexual tension was to masturbate until I achieved that physical release of built up tension.

Now, if I masturbate when I don't have that sexual tension building up, it just has the opposite affect, making me even more sexually frustrated than ever.

I have pretty much figured out I am just feeling a strong desire to be intimate, and of course, at times, that desire is also making me horny, and I get aroused. Then I get sexually frustrated if I am not actually physically horny.

I guess, basically the simplest way for me to explain, is that my emotional and physical states of arousal are so completely out of sync, and at times, it feels like I am ready to climb the walls from frustration.

It really does not help that, though that desire to be intimate seems a little bit like a sexual feeling, and the desire to be intimate with a man is a little sexual, for the most part it does not seem to be.

I find that I want to be closer to all my friends and family, like I really want to hug everybody, and not let go.

I just saw one of my uncles as he had just gotten back to town, and I was a little distracted at the time as I was babysitting my cousin's girls, and I was on the way to the health center. He wanted a hug, and I hugged him, and then I hugged him again because I wanted a hug too (I know that might seem silly, but it is what it is).

I want to hug all my nieces and nephews, and tell them how cute, pretty or handsome they are.

I feel a need for constant, human contact, and I begin to feel so isolated and disconnected without it.

I remember sometime last year at work, we were having coffee in the break room, and the break room was packed, so many had to stand. Someone offered me or someone else (I do not exactly remember) a seat on their lap, and then everyone laughed at the hilarious joke.

Of course, now I would probably sit on a man's lap without hesitation, if offered, just to experience what that intimacy felt like.

I have also been toying with the idea, that for those men who get hung up on continuing on calling me by my old name when it comes time that I am no longer am comfortable with being called by my old name, sitting on their lap and asking them nicely to call me Vanida might illustrate to them that they might start to find it more and more uncomfortable to call me by my old name.

So, all that aside, the root of the problem is that I am longing for that close intimacy with a man, that's just not available to me until I find a man who loves me.

Of course, I get frustrated all over again when I realize that not only will he have to overcome the fact that I was not born a woman, but I would probably constantly driving him to sexual arousal as I would frequently want to touch him, hug him, get him to hold me, to just be close to him, to kiss him, and so on and so forth.

It would be really hard for a man to love me, even if he is okay with me not having been born a woman, I have yet to ever have sex, and I don't really want to until someone has made the commitment to love me for the rest of my life.

In my point of view, that means he has to marry me, and additionally, to conform to Inuit tradition, he would have to live with my parents for a time while I live with his parents.

So any man reading this because I gave him a copy of this journal because I want to get involved with him should understand that though it may seem that I am being cruel, he can understand the decisions I have and are making today, and also see I made them before I knew him.

He will have to understand that, in one form or another, I have been sexually frustrated all my life, and I will continue to be so, and now that I desire that close intimacy that exists between a man and a woman, and when I am given that intimacy, I won't hold back, and I won't feel bad for doing so.

I am just going to go ahead and be a bitch, and go make him give me that attention, though I know it's just going to make him horny, want sex and thoroughly frustrate him sexually.

I am finding that to become a woman is going to become very frustrating, sexually, for myself, and then for any man that comes to love me.

Chapter 16 — Surviving Nunavut

To say moving to Nunavut and making a home for myself is proving difficult would be an understatement.

I had expected a complete lack of support from all levels of the Canadian government and public organizations for returning displaced Inuit to their traditional homeland. What I hadn't expected was the harm some local people would direct against me and that all levels of the Canadian government and public organizations would be completely devoid of any emergency services and that none of the law enforcement agencies in Nunavut would bother to make a reasonable effort to protect Nunavut's residents from harm.

When I moved to Nunavut, I leased land from the Hamlet of Kugluktuk, and I began collecting material in order to eventually build my own home. I purchased two lifts of two by four and I disassembled enough crates to scrounge up enough plywood to have enough material to frame the shell of a house.

When the garage of my bosses duplex burned down, I checked with the public housing corporation about public housing, I was told I did not qualify as I had to have been a resident of Nunavut for two years before I qualified for public assistance of any kind.

I was left with living with family, with no home of my own (which was already the case) and no room for my basic necessities as all I had was a bedroom which was also being used as a storage room.

It did not help that while at school for my first year of my carpentry apprenticeship, the Government of Nunavut considerably shortchanged me on my funding, causing me considerable financial harm, and I have found out that the Government of Nunavut is trying to shortchange all beneficiaries on the funding they have committed to provide.

Actually having no home, and therefore no bills back in Nunavut was the only thing that allowed me to get by while in school, but when I returned home, I found that my boss had to lay me off, as he had not enough work for all his employees.

This did not bode well for me, as I knew finding work in Nunavut, other than construction related work was near impossible, it was reasonable for me to assume that being a vocal critic of the Government of Nunavut, being transgendered, having no home, and having a criminal record would really hurt my chances for employment.

I had already surmised that my days as a carpenter would be limited, as I continued to struggle with joint pain, and as I was going through changes on my journey towards becoming a woman, my stamina was being greatly impaired and I was experiencing more and muscle pain as time passed.

Fortunately, I realized that within the most difficult of problems, usually lay great opportunity, as the time that would pass as I looked for work would be an ideal time to spend working on building a home.

As I had now been living in Nunavut for two years, I now qualified for financial assistance, so I asked the public housing corporation for application forms and how long the waiting list for housing was. When I was told that I would have the lowest priority (single) and that people have been waiting for up to eight years for housing (and still waiting apparently), my hopes were completely crushed.

Though I was drawing employment insurance, I was faced with the problem of having time to work on building a home for myself and eventual family, but spending all my money on living expenses would make that effort harder.

I was spending the weekend at the island on which my parents are building their home, and they happened to have a solution to my problem. They had a large canvas tent in which my dad had insulated with inch and a half Styrofoam insulation that they had used to live in when they had been evicted from their home in the middle of winter when they no longer worked for the government.

We loaded it on my dad's alliak and the following day we proceeded to haul it back to town and to my lot. With the freedom to look for work and work on my home, and have a little bit of money to work towards my goals, things looked very promising indeed.

I proceeded to dig all my storage boxes and crates out of the snow and digging out, sorting and going through all the material I had collected. It had been going quite well, when I realized the two massive piles of plywood I had gathered should have been well revealed from the melting snow already. I went to dig out my plywood and I found small pile of approximately fifteen sheets of plywood.

When all the snow had receded and I tallied up all the missing material, I found that over fifty five sheets of plywood, the vast majority of my four by four lumber, and virtually all the two by four lumber scavenged from crates had been stolen.

All I can say is it still hurts that after collecting enough material to build the exterior shell of my home, someone was actually cruel enough to steal most of it.

With much of the bad weather we had in the spring, and with how depressed I was from losing so much material, I did not get much work done this summer.

I did manage to build a tent frame for my small canvas tent and was able to have a place for my deep freeze, and to store some more of my stuff which had been unprotected from the elements, but eventually the wind and rain began to rip apart the canvas as the tent had been an old tent.

I took the tent of the frame and I sheeted the frame with plywood, and I eventually installed metal roofing I had scrounged up from the garbage dump, built a door, and I actually ended up with a very useful and much needed storage shed.

Over the summer, I had actually turned my tent into a nice comfortable home. I already had a bed and dresser from my parents, I had gotten another dresser from one of my aunts, I put in a couple of small end dressers, I put in my computer desk, and I put a bookshelf into the tent.

Seeing the simplicity of the design of sheeting a tent frame, I built a larger shed, so I would have a place to put all my stuff I have in storage.

When I got a letter in the mail informing me I had an appointment to see the endocrinologist, I couldn't help but be excited, is it meant it was fairly likely I was going to get to start hormones.

Before I left for my appointment, it seemed like everything would be going perfectly for the next while, as I was getting some metal roofing from my dad I could use to roof my buildings, I had collected three twelve volt batteries, ordered a two thousand five hundred watt power inverter, ordered a power supply and charge controller, I would be ordering my first windmill soon, I got a whole bunch of crate plywood and some Styrofoam insulation off my old boss, and I ordered a counter-top clothes washer and counter-top clothes spin dryer.

Chapter 17 — A Joyful Discovery

Even though I was fairly eager to see the endocrinologist to begin hormones, I was not looking forward to returning to the city after the way people reacted on my first trip to the city dressing and living as a woman.

I cringed and was not happy being faced with the prospect of being stared at, laughed at, and having derisive comments directed my way.

You can imagine my surprise when I found that all of that did not happen, and people were being respectful, friendly and courteous towards myself. I was really confused and I had trouble grasping what was going on. Hearing a wolf whistle, followed by an angry tirade that began to the effect of "What the heck (I am paraphrasing) is wrong with you? Etc¡K " in which I did not pay attention to the rest of the tirade, because I was focused on and really shocked someone whistled at me, which also added to my confusion.

When a handsome young man held the door open for me, I am pretty sure I must of turned beet red, considering how hot my face felt.

When I finished with my appointment with the endocrinologist, prescription for estrogen and progesterone in hand, it felt like I was walking on air as I left to go do my shopping for the basic items on my shopping list I needed to pick up in the city.

In the subway station, as I was waiting for the train to go to a convenient area of the city for shopping, I saw a woman who looked like she could have been the older sister of a kid I knew before I moved to Nunavut. She looked at me with a strange expression on her face, and turned away to talk to her friend.

She sounded just like my friend, and then I felt like an idiot for not figuring out she would probably look older and somewhat different after a couple of years. As the train arrived, and everyone began to board, I approached her asking if she was who I thought she was, and lo and behold she was.

She was surprised I knew who she was and surprised that I looked like someone she must know, but she couldn't figure out who. I quickly explained who I had been, and after a quick laugh about almost not recognizing each other, we quickly got caught up about what we each had been up to respectively since I had moved away.

When I had moved away, she and her boyfriend had lost their home, her baby had been taken away by social services and they were struggling to get back on their feet.

I was very happy and pleasantly surprised to find out she had gotten back on their feet, got her baby back, and she was now going to school to become a nurse.

I know so many people who are struggling to find their way in this world, it was great to find someone I knew was getting on their feet and learning to take care of themselves.

I gave her the short version of what I was going through to become a woman, and at one point, when she saw I was comfortable walking in heels, she asked me a question that had totally taken me aback; "So do you enjoy strutting your stuff?"

I kind of meekly answered that I did not think I had the

courage to strut my stuff yet, she laughed, and I just looked at her in confusion. She explained that I was walking in heels, so therefore I was already strutting my stuff. I guess if I had already figured that out, I probably would have struggled with walking in heels, as I probably would have had to deal with being self conscious.

Eventually, I really began to wonder what had suddenly changed to make people react so differently, and when I got back to the boarding home I took a long, hard look in the mirror.

It seems so strange that I spent so much time in the last few months prior, looking in the mirror, wondering what was going to change, that I never even noticed the subtle changes I was undergoing.

I had been treating my face with an intense pulse light hair removal machine, and recently had finished a treatment to my face and removed the all the hair on my face, so my face was quite smooth and hair free.

With all the weight I had lost over the last year, my face and body looked different, and with makeup, jewelry, nice clothes and nice boots I looked a bit female at first glance. To top it off, I had little difficulty putting a beautiful smile on my face, and I was quite mesmerized by how much a happy expression changed my appearance.

I knew my change in appearance was subtle, but I was acting like a woman, dressing like a woman, walking like a woman, so apparently my incongruous appearance did not raise any eyebrows, because I was behaving as to the appearance I was presenting.

That night I felt more at peace and happier than I have ever felt in a long time, and as I had only a little bit of money to spend, I had already picked up the basic necessities on my shopping list, and though I had no spending money left I had the rest of the weekend to enjoy some window shopping.

Even though I did not have any money to spend, I got to window shop until my feet actually hurt, I got to visit one of my aunts, who almost literally did a double take when she first saw me since I had begun my transition to womanhood.

I had such a good time in the city, it did not actually bother me that much when, after the weekend was over, one of my aunts back home called and told me that my shed had been broken into, my quad had been flipped and damaged, and my dad's quad was missing.

I did not have much stuff in my shed as it was yet almost empty, and when machines were stolen in Kugluktuk, there was usually little damage, as the kids were stealing them for joyriding, so I wasn't very concerned, just upset that I was still being targeted by cruel people who seemed to be intent on hurting me.

It turns out I was in for a very nasty surprise when I came home.

Chapter 18 – A Nasty Surprise

On my flight home, I wondered about what damage had been done to my stuff, but since they had only broken into a nearly empty shed, the only worry I had was hoping they had not stolen any of the tools I had been using and had put in that shed.

When I was dropped off at my lot, the first thing I noticed was that the window of the door to my tent was smashed open, and there was dvds, pills and miscellaneous stuff strewn about my lot.

Getting out of the van my knees almost buckled as I saw that whoever had broken into my shed, had returned and broken into my tent.

I put my bags down and I went and looked inside, and I felt completely crushed when I saw that everything was completely ransacked and the tent was severely damaged.

I stopped a few passing people and some neighbors and had them call the police.

As I waited I cried for a bit, completely upset and hurt that when all I had to live in was a tent, and someone was actually cruel enough to take that away from me.

One of my neighbors was a nurse, so I asked her to tell the local mental health care worker what happened and ask him if he could come talk to me since I was extremely upset.

When the RCMP officer arrived he told me he already took pictures of the damage to my shed and I told him they had now broken into my tent.

He left to get his camera to take pictures, and when he returned to do so, I asked him what am I supposed to do since my home was rendered uninhabitable.

He told me to go see the housing corporation and he would give a letter of reference that I was in desperate need of emergency assistance.

The local mental health worker came by and gave me a ride to the post office to let me check my mail and then gave me a ride to the local housing corporation and I had a chance to vent and let out the hurt and pain I was experiencing.

Having been through this song and dance before, I was not surprised when I was told there was no emergency assistance of any sort available from the housing corporation, and there would be nothing they could do to help me.

I told them there had to be something, as a complete lack of emergency services was a complete and total breach of Government levels and public organization's fiduciary duty.

I was referred to see the hamlet and inquire about their crisis center. That turned out to be a dead end as they told me they could not help me as the center was a woman's only shelter.

I then went to the local MLA's office, and I wrote a letter explaining what happened and informing the Government of Nunavut that a complete lack of emergency services was a situation that could no longer be tolerated and would have to be addressed.

That night, I slept on my cousin's couch, not really ideal, but what else do you do when you have nothing else.

The next morning I returned to my lot and I began the slow process of emptying out my tent and inventorying the damages and missing items.

About an hour an a half into the process, I had to stop and take a break, as I was getting very upset again when I had discovered my underwear had been rifled through and a good portion of my panties had been stolen. I really felt violated, and at first I had a real hard time working through that emotion and kept getting real upset.

After taking a break for lunch, I returned to my lot and finished going through my stuff and emptying my tent.

Eventually, when I had a chance to sit down and figure out what was stolen and damaged, I saw most everything I had that had any real value, like my television for example, was stolen or damaged. Without any assistance, it will take me years to recover from the financial impact of the ransacking of my home, so essentially, at that point, I was completely destitute.

Imagine all you have is what little you have brought when you moved here, what little your employer and friends have given you, and what you have built with your own two hands.

Imagine you live in a tent, because that is all that you have for a home, but it is your home nonetheless.

Imagine that someone has already stole a significant amount of your building material you need to build your home.

Imagine that someone ruins your home, making it uninhabitable until you can repair the damage.

It should not be too hard to see how unbelievably cruel and hurtful this is, and I have, and still feel considerable hurt and emotional pain, and I just don't understand how someone was mean enough to take my home away from me.

Chapter 19 — Overcoming Adversity

So what does one do when miscreants take away one's home?

In my case, all I can do is repair the damage, and continue on as before, as there isn't going to be any assistance from any level of government or any public organizations.

When thing I know for sure is, that if you move to Nunavut, especially if you are Inuit, you need to have the help and support of your employer, friends and family, otherwise you will be in serious trouble.

You must also be prepared to live in an area of Canada living in complete poverty, with gangs of children, teens and young adults roaming wild and uncontrolled, in the exact same manner as the children in The Lord of the Flies.

I don't like that my property is constantly being damaged, destroyed or stolen.

I have lost count as to how many times my quad has been stolen, ignition system been screwed with since I installed a hidden kill switch, gas been siphoned out, or it has been outright flipped over or damaged.

Since I have moved here, the local police services have not made any reasonable effort to put a stop to the rampant vandalism and theft.

Since moving here, all public services have completely failed in their fiduciary duty to myself to ensure the rights, privileges, and services any Canadian citizen is entitled to in almost every possible way, and every step of the way I have informed the

Government of Nunavut of said fact.

Throughout Canada, the average Inuk makes half of what the average Canadian makes, and in Nunavut the average Inuk makes a third of what the average Nunavut resident makes, a disturbing fact that points out how much the Inuit people are hurting throughout Canada, and especially in Nunavut.

I have lots of family in Nunavut, so I knew this before moving to Nunavut, but I truly underestimated how difficult it would be.

Unfortunately, once here, there was no turning back, and the only thing I could to in my present predicament, is to move forward.

That evening I emptied my tent, I began to disassemble it in order to work on it and restore it to a habitable condition with the help of my cousin, and we restructured and rebuilt the floor.

Later that week, I dropped by the MLA's office and they put me in touch with him, and I asked what they intended to do about the complete lack of emergency housing. He interrogated me on what I have done to remedy my circumstances (which I told him), he assured me he would see to it that something was done about my situation, and I informed him that my primary concern was that the Nunavut Government would remedy the lack of emergency housing, though I would appreciate assistance.

The MLA was quite adversarial in our conversation, so my experience tells me the Government of Nunavut will be working hard to keep what is happening in Nunavut hidden to avoid liability, instead of giving me a little bit of help.

I feel good about what I have accomplished since my home was ransacked, as I have rebuilt my tent into a small cabin, and I am currently building a workshop so I will have a place to work on my quad and snowmobile to restore them to good working order.

Additionally, I have been fortunate to have the aid and support of my friends and family, as there has been no shortage of adversity for me to overcome since moving to Nunavut.

It has been frustrating moving to a third world state, but it is what it is, and I am just going to make the best of my situation and continue to work towards building a good home for myself, and hopefully someday I will have a family to share what I am building with.

Chapter 20 – The End of the Beginning

I really thought that transitioning from male to female was going to consume a huge portion of my life, but now that I have started down the path, I find myself really surprised that it has not been the case.

As I have written before, it feels like I have been becoming a new being, but in reality I have just been becoming myself again, and now it is just life as usual.

Aside from slowly changing my body, the biggest change in my life is that I am not completely miserable, and I really look forward to all the good things in life, and it is much easier to work towards building a home for myself and eventual family.

The biggest thing I learned was that it was not necessary to become a woman to stop being miserable.

Wanting to be a woman is simply one of the many things I want that are part of what all my hopes and dreams consist of. Becoming a woman is not something I need, pursuing my hopes and dreams are what I need.

I will forever after be happy if I work towards the things I want, and eventually I will start to attain many of the things my heart desires.

I hope I will find a man who loves me, who treats me kindly and respectfully.

I will have children, to love, to protect and to provide guidance to.

I will build a home for myself and my family.

I will always have the opportunity to tinker, to build and to create to my hearts contentment.

There will always be people whom I love and care about to share what's on my mind.

There is nothing to stop me from writing whatsoever I want, and there is nothing to stop me from sharing my writings to anyone who will listen.

I won't always have the work I want, but I will always enjoy and be content with whatever I do.

I have friends and family whom I love, and who love me, no matter what I do.

I wear whatever I want, I wear the clothes that I find comfortable, and I will always enjoy dressing up in the clothes that make me feel good about myself.

I enjoy shopping, looking for the necessities of life, and looking at, browsing and enjoying what the world has to offer.

I am healthy, I am joyful, and I enjoy the wonders of daily life.

I have the rest of my life to learn all the things I desire to learn and have yet to learn.

I look forward to having a family, to spending the rest of my life to share my love with, to take care of, to provide for.

So many of the things that my heart desired, became mine when I started being myself.

Not that long ago I thought by working towards the things I

wanted, the hopes and dreams in my heart, I would be happy.

At this point Vanida's Journey is no longer about me becoming a woman, it is about the start of a journey, the path I walk as part of enjoying a happy and fulfilling life, a path I refused to walk for so long.

I no longer travel the road to misery, but it is not easy path as it is full of challenges, hardship and hurdles to overcome. It is, however, rewarding and fulfilling, now, and forever.

Epilogue – A Hard Home

As I have stated before, I was a little bit surprised by the fact that my desire to become a woman stopped consuming me and taking up my entire life, but when I think about it, I should not have been.

The only reason that desire consumed me and made me so miserable was because I was burying it and trying to suppress it, and it was an important part of myself.

When I stopped suppressing that desire, and I began to truly believe I could become a woman, I no longer had anything to be concerned about in respect to becoming a woman.

There are definitely steps I have to take on the path to transitioning from male to female, but they are quite infrequent as the process is deliberately slow to allow someone such as myself to not make hasty decisions I would regret.

Nowadays, the things on my mind that bother me consist of concern for a lack of having a home, stress about finding employment, desire and longing for a mate, and all the pain and misery I witness in the community I live in.

As I have found, Nunavut is a harsh place to make a home in, and I am fortunate to have much help from my friends and family, which allows me to continue on and move forward in my life.

As I have encountered the hurdles that make life so harsh in Nunavut, I have regularly endeavored to inform and point these things out to Nunavut's politicians and our Government, but unfortunately, I am attacked and sometimes ostracized for doing so.

As harsh as the home I chose to live in is to survive in, I have found it to be a beautiful land, and that it is a land the Creator gave us which had, and still has the ability to take care of our needs in every way.

Knowing the Inuit peoples thrived in these lands long before modern civilization came along allows me to look to the past to figure out how to survive in our modern age in Nunavut.

Epilogue, Again (P.P.S.)

It has been over a month since I contacted my local MLA for help and it looks like the Government won't give me the time of the day to let me know how (or if) they plan to address the very serious concerns I have brought up.

In addition, in a position of employment I applied for with the Government Of Nunavut, where I was well qualified, experienced, and submitted a sample of my work with the application, I was not even considered for the position. Additionally, when I appealed the decision to not consider me for an interview, the Government Of Nunavut did not give me an opportunity to attend the appeal hearing or appoint a representative to attend on my behalf, and the concerns I brought up in my appeal were not addressed.

Though that may not sound unusual in itself, the Government Of Nunavut's own policy, and it's fiduciary duty imposed by the Nunavut Land Claims Agreement, require them to give beneficiaries such as myself priority consideration for all available employment, and any hearing of any kind cannot be considered fair, if the appellant does not have opportunity to state her case, or especially if none of her concerns brought up in the appeal were addressed by the appeal.

I am not all that surprised, as most of all the people I know in Nunavut have informed me that the Government Of Nunavut rarely awards an employment position to an Inuk, except when the rejection is appealed and the applicant is either exceedingly qualified, or are known to fall in line with all the attitudes and perspectives of the Nunavut Government.

In fact, everyone I know who have worked to promote change in our government have been demoted, ostracized or wrongfully dismissed.

I am not worried, however, as the time I have available to me while I look for work allows me to get a good start on the next book I am working on, which I am tentatively calling "Failing Nunavut", where I write about the hurdles, hardships and ordeals I have found the modern Inuit people are facing, and I also go into detail on many of the ways they are overcoming adversity in Nunavut.

About The Author

As you already know, my name is Vanida Corazon Kemaktun Plamondon, born Vernon Richard Paul Plamondon, and I was born in, and grew up in a small town in the Northwest Territories called Fort Smith.

My father came from a small town in Alberta called Plamondon, and my mother came from Kugluktuk, where they currently reside, and are slowly building their home, where they plan to retire.

I have made Kugluktuk my home, and though I have second thoughts sometimes, I don't regret moving here. I imagine, however, due to my outspoken nature, there are many who don't appreciate me moving here.

That is not going to change, as I enjoy writing and expressing what's on my mind, and it's easiest to write about what I know, so look forward to more books in the near future.

Other than a couple of minor details, I am a rather ordinary person, with truly ordinary goals, hopes and dreams. That, however, does not make my thoughts, ideas or opinions irrelevant, and I am sure that the thoughts, ideas and opinions of an ordinary woman are as interesting to the masses as any others.

Thank you for reading my book. If you are interested in sending feedback or wish to contact me, I can be contacted at vanida.plamondon@gmail.com, and if you appreciated my book and you would like to help me out financially by sending me a dollar (or any other amount), you can do so via PayPal using the same email address.

Attribution-NonCommercial-NoDerivatives Canada 2.5, License

License

THE WORK (AS DEFINED BELOW) IS PROVIDED UNDER THE TERMS OF THIS CREATIVE COMMONS PUBLIC LICENSE (hereafter "LICENSE"). THE WORK IS PROTECTED BY COPYRIGHT AND/OR OTHER APPLICABLE LAW. ANY USE OF THE WORK OTHER THAN AS AUTHORIZED UNDER THIS LICENSE IS PROHIBITED.

BY EXERCISING ANY RIGHTS TO THE WORK PROVIDED HERE, YOU ACCEPT AND AGREE TO BE BOUND BY THE TERMS OF THIS LICENSE. THE LICENSOR GRANTS YOU THE RIGHTS CONTAINED HERE IN CONSIDERATION OF YOUR ACCEPTANCE OF SUCH TERMS AND CONDITIONS.

(1) Definitions.

(1.01) "Collective Work" means a work, such as a dictionary, yearbook, encyclopedia, or a newspaper, review magazine or singular periodical and any work written in distinct parts by different authors, or in which works or parts of works of different authors are incorporated. A work that constitutes a Collective Work will not be considered a Derivative Work (as defined below) for the purposes of this license.

(1.02) "Derivative Work" means a work that produces or reproduces the Work or any substantial part thereof in any material form. Derivative works include:

(1.02 A) Translations of the Work;

(1.02 B) Where the Work is a dramatic work, conversions of the Work into a novel or other non-dramatic work;

(1.02 C) Where the Work is a novel or other non-dramatic work or an artistic work, conversions of the Work into a dramatic work by way of performance in public or otherwise;

(1.02 D) Where the Work is a literary or dramatic or musical work, making a sound recording, cinematographic film or other mechanical contrivance by means of which the

Work may be mechanically reproduced or performed; and

(1.02 E) Where the Work is a literary or dramatic or musical or artistic work, reproductions, adaptations or public presentations of the Work as a cinematographic work.

A work that constitutes a Collective Work will not be considered a Derivative Work for the purpose of this License. Where the Work is a musical composition or sound recording, the synchronization of the Work in time-relation with a moving image (IE. cinematographic work "syncing") will be treated as a Derivative Work for the purpose of this License.

(1.03) "License Elements" means the following high-level License attributes as selected by Licensor and indicated in the title of this License: Attribution, Noncommercial, NoDerivatives, ShareAlike.

(1.04) "Licensor" means the individual or entity that offers the Work under the terms of this License.

(1.05) "Moral Rights" means rights that an individual who creates a Work protected by copyright has concerning the integrity of the work, the attribution (or anonymity) of authorship, and the right not to be associated with a product, service, cause or institution, or rights of similar nature in the Work anywhere in the world.

(1.06) "Musical Work" means any work of music or musical composition, with or without words, and includes any compilation thereof.

(1.07) "Original Author" means the individual who created the Work.

(1.08) "Use" means to exercise one or more of the rights set out below as granted by the License and includes the title thereof when such title is original and distinctive.

(1.08 A) to produce or reproduce the work in any material form;

(1.08 B) to perform the work in public;

(1.08 C) if the work is unpublished, to publish the work;

(1.08 D) to convert a dramatic work into a non-dramatic work;

(1.08 E) to convert a non-dramatic work into a dramatic work;

(1.08 F) to make a sound recording, cinematographic film or other contrivance by means of which the work may be mechanically reproduced or performed;

(1.08 G) to reproduce, adapt and publicly present the work, as a cinematographic film;

(1.08 H) to communicate the work to the public by telecommunication;

(1.08 I) to present at a public exhibition, for a purpose other than sale or hire, an artistic work created after June 7, 1988, other than a map, chart or plan;

(1.08 J) to rent a computer program;

(1.08 K) to rent a sound recording embodying a musical work; and/or

(1.08 L) to authorize such acts.

(1.09) "Work" means the distinctive and original work of authorship offered under the terms of this License.

(1.10) "You" means an individual or entity exercising rights under this License who has not previously violated the terms of this License with respect to the Work, or who has received express permission from the Licensor to exercise rights under this License despite a previous violation.

(2) Fair Dealing Rights. Nothing in this license is intended to reduce, limit, or restrict any rights accruing to fair dealing, and those exemptions afforded to individuals, educational institutions, libraries, archives, museums, computer programs, incidental inclusions and ephemeral recordings, or other limitations on the exclusive rights of the copyright owner under the Copyright Act.

(3) License Grant. Subject to the terms and conditions of this License, Licensor hereby grants You a worldwide, royalty-free, non-exclusive, perpetual (for the duration of the applicable copyright) License to exercise the rights in the Work as stated below:

(3.01) to Use the Work, to incorporate the Work into one or more Collective Works, and to Use the Work as incorporated in the Collective Works.

The above rights may be exercised in all media and formats whether now known or hereafter devised. The above rights include the right to make such modifications as are technically necessary to exercise the rights in other media and formats.

All rights not expressly granted by Licensor are hereby reserved, including but not limited to the rights set forth in Section 4(b) and 4(d).

Except as otherwise agreed by the Original Author, if You Use a Work or any Derivative Works or Collective Works in any material form, You must not do anything that would offend the Moral Rights of the Original Author, including but not limited to:

(3.01 A) You must not falsely attribute the Work to someone other than the Original Author; and

(3.01 B) If applicable, You must respect the Original Author's wish to remain anonymous or pseudonymous.

All other moral rights are waived. This means the Original Author is not reserving the ability to prevent downstream creators from engaging in material distortion or modification of the work, including, but limited to, associating the Work with a particular product, service, cause or institution.

(4) Restrictions. The license granted in Section 3 above is expressly made subject to and limited by the following restrictions:

(4.01) You may Use the Work only under the terms of this License, and You must include a copy of, or the Uniform Resource Identifier for, this License with every copy or sound recordings of the Work You Use. You may not offer or impose any terms on the Work that alter or restrict the terms of this or the recipients' exercise of the rights granted hereunder. You may not sub-license the Work. You must keep intact all notices that refer to this License and to the disclaimer of warranties. You may not Use the Work with any technological measures that control access or use of the Work in a manner inconsistent with the terms of this License Agreement.

The above applies to the Work as incorporated in a Collective Work, but this does not require the Collective Work apart from the Work itself to be made subject to the terms of this License.

If You create a Collective Work, upon request from any Licensor You must, to the extent practicable, include or remove from the Collective Work any credit required by clause 4.03.

(4.02) You may not exercise any of the rights granted to You in Section 3 above in any manner that is primarily intended for or directed toward commercial advantage or private monetary compensation. The exchange of the Work for other copyrighted works by means of digital file-sharing or otherwise shall not be considered to be intended for or directed toward commercial advantage or private monetary compensation, provided there is no payment of any monetary compensation in connection with the exchange of copyrighted works.

(4.03) If you Use the Work or Collective Works, You must keep intact all copyright notices for the Work and give the Original Author credit reasonable to the medium or means You are utilizing to the (i) Original Author by using his, her or its name (or pseudonym) if supplied; and/or (ii) if the Original Author and/or Licensor designate another party or parties (eg. a sponsor institution, publishing entity, journal) for attribution in Licensor's copyright notice or terms of service or by other reasonable means, then to such party or parties; the title of the Work if supplied; to the extent reasonably practicable, the Uniform Resource Identifier, if any, that Licensor specifies to be associated with the Work, unless such URI does not refer to the copyright notice or licensing information for the Work. Such credit may be implemented in any reasonable manner; provided, however, that in the case of a Collective Work, at a minimum such credit will appear where any other comparable authorship credit appears and in a manner at least as prominent as such other comparable authorship credit.

(4.04) For the avoidance of doubt, where the Work is a musical composition, performer's performance or sound recording:

(4.04 a) Performance Royalties Under Blanket Licenses. Licensor reserves the exclusive right to collect, whether individually or via a performance rights society, royalties for the public performance or public digital performance (e.g. webcast) of the musical Work, sound recording or performer's performance if that performance is primarily intended for or directed toward commercial advantage or private monetary compensation.

(4.04 b) Mechanical Rights in Musical Works. Licensor reserves the exclusive right to collect, whether individually or via a music rights agency, collective society, or designated agent, royalties for any sound recording You create from the musical Work ("cover version") if Your Use of such cover version is primarily intended for or directed toward commercial advantage or private monetary compensation.

(5) Representations, Warranties and Disclaimer. UNLESS OTHERWISE MUTUALLY AGREED TO BY THE PARTIES IN WRITING, LICENSOR OFFERS THE WORK AS-IS AND MAKES NO REPRESENTATIONS OR WARRANTIES OF ANY KIND CONCERNING THE WORK, EXPRESS, IMPLIED, STATUTORY OR OTHERWISE, INCLUDING, WITHOUT LIMITATION, WARRANTIES OF TITLE, MERCHANTIBILITY, FITNESS FOR A PARTICULAR PURPOSE, NONINFRINGEMENT, OR THE ABSENCE OF LATENT OR OTHER DEFECTS, ACCURACY, OR THE PRESENCE OF ABSENCE OF ERRORS, WHETHER OR NOT DISCOVERABLE. SOME JURISDICTIONS DO NOT ALLOW THE EXCLUSION OF IMPLIED WARRANTIES, SO SUCH EXCLUSION MAY NOT APPLY TO YOU.

(6) Limitation on Liability. EXCEPT TO THE EXTENT REQUIRED BY APPLICABLE LAW, AND EXCEPT FOR DAMAGES ARISING FROM LIABILITY TO A THIRD PARTY RESULTING FROM BREACH OF THE WARRANTIES IN SECTION 5, IN NO EVENT WILL LICENSOR BE LIABLE TO YOU ON ANY LEGAL THEORY FOR ANY SPECIAL, INCIDENTAL, CONSEQUENTIAL, PUNITIVE OR EXEMPLARY DAMAGES ARISING OUT OF THIS LICENSE OR THE USE OF THE WORK, EVEN IF LICENSOR HAS BEEN ADVISED OF THE POSSIBILITY OF SUCH DAMAGES.

(7) Termination.

(7.01) This License and the rights granted hereunder will terminate automatically upon any breach by You of the terms of this License. Individuals or entities who have received Collective Works from You under this License, however, will not have their licenses terminated provided such individuals or entities remain in full compliance with those licenses. Sections 1, 2, 5, 6, 7, and 8 will survive any termination of this License.

(7.02) Subject to the above terms and conditions, the license granted here is perpetual (for the duration of the applicable copyright in the Work). Notwithstanding the above, Licensor reserves the right to release the Work under different license terms or to stop distributing the Work at any time; provided, however that any such election will not serve to withdraw this License (or any other license that has been, or is required to be, granted under the terms of this License), and this License will continue in full force and effect unless terminated as stated above.

(8) Miscellaneous.

(8.01) Each time You Use the Work or a Collective Work, the Licensor offers to the recipient a license to the Work on the same terms and conditions as the license granted to You under this License.

(8.02) If any provision of this License is invalid or unenforceable under applicable law, it shall not affect the validity or enforceability of the remainder of the terms of this License, and without further action by the parties to this agreement, such provision shall be reformed to the minimum extent necessary to make such provision valid and enforceable.

(8.03) No term or provision of this License shall be deemed waived and no breach consented to unless such waiver or consent shall be in writing and signed by the party to be charged with such waiver or consent.

(8.04) This License constitutes the entire agreement between the parties with respect to the Work licensed here. There are no understandings, agreements or representations with respect to the Work not specified here. Licensor shall not be bound by any additional provisions that may appear in any communication from You. This License may not be modified without the mutual written agreement of the Licensor and You.

(8.05) You must abide the License during its term despite the expiry, initial invalidity or later invalidation of any intellectual property rights.

(8.06) The construction, validity and performance of this License shall be governed by the laws in force in Canada and, where applicable, those of the province in which the Licensor normally resides.

9 780987 843807